POETRY FROM BENGAL

The Delta Rising

An anthology of Modern Bengali poetry

Translated by
RON D.K. BANERJEE

FOREST BOOKS/UNESCO
LONDON ☆ 1989 ☆ BOSTON

UNESCO COLLECTION OF REPRESENTATIVE WORKS
Series UNESCO Library of World Poetry

Published by
FOREST BOOKS

20 Forest View, Chingford, London E4 7AY, U.K.
PO Box 438 Wayland, MA 01778, U.S.A.

First published 1989

Typeset in Great Britain by Cover to Cover, Cambridge
Printed in Great Britain by BPCC Wheatons Ltd, Exeter

British Library Cataloguing in Publication Data
Poetry from Bengal: The Delta Rising
— (UNESCO world poetry library series (1945–1985))
1. Poetry in Bengali, 1940– — Anthologies — English texts
I. Series
891'.4417'08

ISBN 0–948259–79–5

Library of Congress Catalog Card Number

89–85179

In memory of my mother Amola
and my father Pramatha Nath Banerjee of Calcutta
and in gratitude for their gift of life and language.

The following translations were published in the magazines cited below:

International Poetry Review Spring 1981
Holderlin' by Buddhadev Bose; 'In Memory of the Poet Dilip Kumar Sen', 'In the Temple' by Sakti Chattopadhyaya; 'Ice Age' by Sunil Gangopadhyaya; 'Banalata Sen' by Jibanananda Das; 'O Life', 'Convoy', 'Graffiti' by Sukanta Bhattacharya; 'Irrelevant' by Vijaya Mukhopadhyaya; 'You are Sunward' by Kabirul Islam.

The Harvard Advocate Special Translation Issue, Summer 1982
'Night' by Jibanananda Das; 'Calcutta's Jesus' by Nirendranath Chakravarty; 'Nowadays' by Tushar Roy.

Translation, Translation Centre, Columbia University, Fall 1982
'The Empty Space' by Vijaya Mukhopadhyaya

Translation, Columbia University, Spring 1983
'Death's Hand' by Nirendranath Chakravarty; 'The Naked Solitary Hand' by Jibanananda Das; 'Company' by Vijaya Mukhopadhyaya.

Contents

Preface

Poetry confers both a habitation and a name on all it touches. If naming is individuation, it is also an evocation of universals. For name is the most fundamental of conventions, as Shakespeare knew. And conventions (from *convenire*) bring together. Thus the past flows into the poetry of the present through the very medium of language, in conventions which preserve echoes of *temps perdu* and mark it as articulation of a special kind. But such diachronicity does not suffice to define poetry. In its synchronic aspect, specific contexts, customs and forms, politics and history, particularly geography with nature for its symbolic dimension, give it the urgency of immediacy. The land that gives the poet birth always underlies the landscape of his emotions. Modern Bengali poetry, with a thousand years of literature behind it, is no exception. It tussles with the ghosts of its forbears, looks to shape the future against the background of a landscape that lends it concreteness and individuality.

Even now, after the trauma of Partition and the attendant diminution, in not only physical but cultural terms, Bengal holds a unique place on the Indian subcontinent. It is a land and culture of interstices, a grid which holds opposites in tension. Physically, the Himalayas tower in its north, from which the rivers criss-cross their way to the south and the sea. There lies the fertile delta formed by, among others, the tributaries of the Ganges, with immemorial forests on their shifting banks or the paddy fields which change from green to gold with the cycle of the seasons. To the west stretches the sweeping Indo-Gangetic plain — *aryavarta* (the land of the Aryans); to the east, the present Bangladesh and further on, the frontiers of Burma. Fishing boats with bright sails ply the rivers from a thousand arpeggios of islands at the confluence of the delta with the Bay of Bengal.

This landscape, a splendid quilt of many colours, offers its counterpart in a culture of great complexity and variety, sometimes in bold themes, sometimes in muted nuances.

The pre-Indo-Aryan traditions here cross-bred with the Brahmanical traditions of its Aryan conquerers, whose ultimate triumph lies in the fact that Bengali is a daughter language of Sanskrit. But Buddhism, too, found a congenial home among the indigenous people, who never took to the Aryan caste system. Deepankar Srijnana converted Tibet from the matrix of Bengali Buddhism. With its cult of goddesses, in its passionate response to the sensual and the physical, which no Aryan Monism could subjugate, Bengal also gave birth to what Heinrich Zimmer has characterised as the most brilliant Metaphysical system of the Indian middle ages, namely Tantrism. As the etymology of *tantra* indicates, *tanu* (body), in this system, is the vehicle for crossing over (*tri*) into transcendence. This refusal to abandon the physical world and the concreteness of life informs all great Bengali poetry, such as in the imagery of medieval Vaishnava poetry, centring on the love between Radha and the god Krishna. The great Vaishnava celebration of *eros* as the lyrical vehicle of *agape*, whether in the *Gitagovinda* of Jayadeva, the last great poet in Sanskrit, in Vidyapathi's Maithili lyrics or in the poems of Chandidas or Govindadas in the vernacular, has left an indelible mark on Bengali sensibility, not merely on poetic conventions. And that is equally true of the Sahajiya and the Baul songs, in which the actual landscape comes alive in images of diurnal rounds and stands in tension with the mystical wanderer's ecstatic cries. The poems in *Poetry from Bengal* resonate in varying degrees to this complex tradition, even when trying to elude it. Vishnu Dey, for example, deploys images drawn from the Vaishnava poets in his love poetry, but locates them in a contemporary setting.

The poems presented in this volume are a selection and by no means representative of even contemporary Bengali poetry which, with its long history, flows in many powerful currents. The poets of Bangladesh, who also write in Bengali, are excluded, not by my choice, but for reasons of political, not cultural boundaries. But even among the others, Rabindranath Tagore, Bengal's greatest poet, the poet-composer Dwijendralal Roy, the fiery Nazrul Islam, the technically masterful Satyen Dutta, all are missing from this volume. The poets I have presented here are Modernists, whereas those just mentioned, no matter their achievements, are not. And the Modernists, little known abroad, have also written brilliant poetry that deserves attention. Their achievements dominate the present and anticipate the future.

By a modernist poet I mean one who set out to change the conventions governing Bengali literature and the world-view it embodied. Of course, their aims and approaches varied. But they are all self-conscious innovators who put traditional literary, social, political and moral values into question. And the matrix from which their questioning rises is a new urban sensibility of a developing technological age, with an attendant awareness of alienation, of persistent poverty as an economic — not foreordained — fact, of dehumanization. Not that they are poets of doom, but they all share a sense of 'endings' in different ways. Dines Das' or Sukanta Bhattacharya's poems illustrate these themes very well. Nationalism is common to almost all Bengali poets since the turn of the century, modernist or not, and it does not provide a line of demarcation.

By contrast, Tagore's poetry does not engage this new sensibility, although he was acutely aware of the contemporary scene. Nor do Nazrul's incandescent lyrics or Satyendranath Dutta's brilliant rhythmic arabesques. There is an absence of focus on the concrete thinginess of life in their poetry, even though there is no absence of specificity. The enthusiastic adoption of the free verse also sets the Modernists apart. For most of them, the free verse is a more pliant, apt instrument for representing the fast changing world around them, in bringing poetry in contact with the spoken language. That, of course, does not mean that they only write in free verse or that all of them wrote in it. Sudhindranath Dutta, for example, preferred more formal verse and deliberately avoided idiom and slang in favour of a high diction that resonates to the classical tradition. Nevertheless, his sensibility, imagery, his irony mark him a modern poet. And the impact of prose, creative or critical, which is felt in the free verse form, is perceptible in his poetry as well. His poem 'Doubt', for example, draws on the erotic metaphors of Sanskrit poetry, but only as a counterpoint to his own, culled from ordinary life, which undercut the hyperboles.

The Bengali modernists adopted the free verse mainly from the West. But theirs was no blind imitation. Eliot has noted the beat of the alexandrine beneath the *vers libre* of St. John Perse in *Anabase*. Equally, the traditional Bengali metres beat below the modern Bengali free verse poems, such as Jivanananda Das'. Tagore, on the other hand, rejected free verse and stuck to more formally patterned rhymed verse, like Yeats. I agree with critics like Sankha Ghosh that his experiments with free verse show a misunderstanding of the form. But, in his hands, the old forms gain new vitality. And new rhythmic and stanzaic patterns were created by him to overcome rigidities of the old forms. Similarly, Nazrul Islam's odes show freedom from traditional constraints in their deployment of rhyme and rhythm and Satyen Dutta's metrical innovations are a mark of his expressive originality. I have included several more formal poems, such as sonnets, by the Modernists to show their handling of traditional forms.

In his preface to *The Best Poems of One Year* (1974), Manindra Gupta speculated that at least two thousand poets had published over ten thousand poems in various Bengali magazines just that year. That gives an idea of the task facing any anthologist of modern Bengali poetry, who tries to make a representative selection. But more importantly, it points to the centrality of the poetic tradition in Bengali culture, even in these days when poetry brings neither prestige nor profit. For in Calcutta, public readings of poetry are still held before packed halls, to which men and women come from the streets. They pay entrance fees which are considerable, given the earning power of the average Bengali. And, not only do they render the poets the tribute of rapt attention during the readings, they participate fully in the ensuing discussions of poetry from the floor. Used to small, elite audiences in university circles in the USA or Europe, I have often felt surprised and moved by their spontaneous enthusiasm for this the most ancient of expressive forms.

This centrality of the poetic tradition calls for an effort to keep an unbroken link between the street and the study on the part of both the poet and the public. Even the Modernist movement, while leaving its readers bewildered at times, never looks down on the public, as it tries to reshape the very conventions that articulate their sensibility. There is little desire for *épater le bourgeois* in its poetics; and the public knows its inclusive intent. So there is the charming and useful custom of presenting books of verse on various special occasions, such as marriages, birthdays and anniversaries. In such small but significant ways, the public responds by acknowledging the role that poetry can play in ordinary life. And the precarious continuum of social discourse, of thought and feeling, that underlies literature — *sahitya* or togetherness in Bengali — seems to survive the cacophony of political and other controversies. The ideal of interaction between different levels of speech in many voices, which the Modernists experimented with, still seems to be there, if attenuated by the corrosive alienation that marks the Modernist phenomenon everywhere. The paradox of the poet being the more alienated when trying to be more engaged is present in the modern Bengali literary scene also.

Now to give a brief sketch of the background. Tagore wrote in *My Life* (1928) about the inward and outward thrusts of Bengali literature at the time of his birth in 1861. The Bengali renaissance, which had begun with Raja Rammohan Roy in the early nineteenth century, was in full swing by this time. As Tagore has noted, it involved a massive reevaluation of the interrelated spheres of the religious, social and literary traditions and, thereby, of national identity. Since the British presence had provided both a challenge and an impetus, in their introspection and retrospection about the past, the Bengali intellectuals and poets, from the beginning, remained simultaneously engaged with the claims and values of Western culture. Michael Madhusudhan Dutt, the most important Bengali poet of the time, best exemplifies this sort of dialogue. He imported the sonnet and the blank verse from English literature and, in his dramatic-epic *Meghnadvadhkavya*, recast old myths with ironic vigour and psychological depth. In his hand, as in Hemchandra's and later in Tagore's, classical myths came to provide dramatic opportunities and not merely to serve as vehicles for an age-old, accretive system of values. Eventually, the old myths would turn into symbols and stand side by side with new myths drawn from history, especially with the Modernists. Jivanananda Das' 'Banalata Sen', thus draws on the Upanishads as well as Indian history in creating its imaginative landscape.

Also, as Sankha Ghosh points out in *Chhander Varanda*, Michael M. Dutt made the word stand on its own, separating it from music and so initiated the line of later development in Bengali poetry. His blank verse (*amitrakhshara*) anticipates the free verse, even though Miltonic in inspiration. Again, the introduction of detailed punctuation marks at this time, under the influence of English, indicates a shift in the very syntax of thought towards the analytical mode.

Of course, in Tagore's poetry — with *motz et son* in intimate unity, with new cadences and rhythms, new tonalities echoing common speech — the millenial tradition finds a triumphant rebirth. Yet, it was a precarious triumph. Modern life demanded new forms, new language, freer rhythms. That Tagore, after resisting free verse for years, like Yeats, should try his hand at it in the end is both a tribute to his versatility and openness and an acknowledgement of the changing times. Even today, Rabindranath Tagore remains the most loved and widely known poet of Bengal, and not the least for his thousands of songs, but his attempt to make the received tradition new seems to have failed.

Tagore's creative career, spanning some sixty years, until his death in 1941, marks an epoch all on its own. His poetry has drawn on all the sources and genres of the Bengali poetic tradition, from the great Vaishnava lyrics of the Middle Ages to folk-songs and tales, from the Classical Sanskrit poetry of Kalidasa and the erotic poetry of Bharatchandra to the epics and the puranas, from history, the *Jatakas,* from the Baul's songs of the path to the devotional songs of Ramprasada. The encyclopedic range of his poetry is truly amazing. And only Victor Hugo shows comparable creative energy and versatility in the modern Western tradition. Of course, one recalls Gide's ambiguous response, 'Victor Hugo. Hélas!', when asked who was the greatest of the French poets. And there are those who would echo that about Tagore. But his stature as a great poet stands secure.

The Modernist movement, in some ways, began as a struggle against Tagore's immense influence. And the pioneers often looked to the Modernist poets and movements in the West for inspiration. Yeats, Eliot, Pound (who had introduced Tagore to America through Harriet Weaver's *Poetry* magazine), later on Auden, Stevens, to cite a few, all have had an impact on modern Bengali poetry, as also the French Symbolists, Hölderlin, Heine, Rilke, not to mention Dante, Milton, Goethe and others in new interpretations. Buddhadeva Bose, to take one of the pioneers of Modernism in the twenties, aggressively looked westward both in his poetry and criticism. His poems, 'Hölderlin' and 'Icarus' testify to his interest and to his brilliant power of assimilation. Just as his criteria for Bengali Modernism resonate to the culture of manifestos of the *avantgarde* movements in the West. But he was, by no means, the only one to draw inspiration from other shores.

What later became Modernism in poetry finds its genesis, as I have mentioned, in a larger attempt to consider the Indian identity in the context of a developing industrial age, in terms of a dialogue between the ancient and the modern. Perforce, thanks to the British presence, that implicated different geographical as well as linguistic horizons. The 'bilingual' poetry of Tushar Roy with its jazzy rhythms or the composite imaginative landscape in Buddhadev Bose's 'My tower' attests to this point of confluence. Even today, in post-independence Calcutta, one is impressed by the cosmopolitanism of its intellectuals and poets. But a certain deliberate parochialism seems to cast a creeping shadow. Yet, if the spaceship earth grows smaller with time, the Bengali poets seem to take that into account. And panhumanism underlies even the most concrete poems rooted in the specific contours of a culture or place, such as Samsul Haque's 'Into the newborn's hands'. To portray this cosmopolitan dimension of Bengali poetry, I have deliberately chosen certain poems which consciously engage it. Vishnu Dey's 'Paul Robeson', Premen Mitra's 'George Bernard Shaw', or Buddha Bose's 'Hölderlin' are obvious examples. But Nabaneeta Dev Sen's 'One day, like Gregor Samsa', no less, provides a complex metaphorical transparency in its title.

The poems in this collection are translations from some thirty poets, spanning the period from the 1920s to the present. I have chosen them primarily for their merit. But their representative quality, in giving a sense of Bengali life with its cultural vigour and diversity, was also an important consideration. I have tried to be scrupulously faithful to the original poems, but not at the cost of their poetic value when read in English. Bengali metres or even cadences are not for the most part reproduceable in English. Even line divisions involve a different rhythm. Some of Jivanananda's lines, to cite an example, contain as many as forty-two syllables, creating an impression of rivers meandering on the page. I have eschewed the temptation of reproducing such implicit images.

I have accepted formal constraints when translating poems in defined verse forms — a sonnet, for example. But I do not subscribe to the literalist theory of translation which implies that a poem is reified on the page. Nor do I accept the Crocean theory of the untranslatability of poetry which, from the opposite point of view, posits the same view. *Traduttore, traditore,* says the Italian adage. But not if the translator remains loyal to the authenticity of the original, the power that had moved him in the first place. For a poem exists in the act of reading, not merely on the page. And, if truly vibrant, it is recreated with each reading, as its subliminal possibilities take life in the reader's mind, in new shapes, around what William Frost calls its pillar symbols. A translation, if it is also a poem, is no different. It is a bridge to alien shores, which become familiar when we have crossed over. Whether one calls it translation, transcreation or imitation makes little difference.

Ron D.K. Banerjee
Five College Institute,
Amherst, Massachussetts

The Poems

ARCHANA ACHARYACHOWDHURY

(1941—)

Mrs Acharyachowdhury teaches at Rishi Bankim College in Naihati, West Bengal, and has published poetry in various magazines. 'Chimera' appeared in Ek Bacharer Sreshtha Kavita (ed. Manindra Gupta and Ranjit Sinha), Calcutta 1975.

Chimera

A yellow viper slides
    through glass blades.
A frog's piteous scream
    rang out.
By the stagnant pond,
the banyan roots
are a woman ascetic's
matted hair.
    Your face, seen in dreams,
was limned
in dusty clouds.

We swim, we dolphins,
dive down,
surfacing in intimacy.
Libido's dead fish
    drift
    in tortuous currents.
It was I
who broke up our tender
water frolics.

From the black-yellow viper
comes a keen hiss
of pain.
You had set it on fire
    and then
clutched it
    with both hands.
Love was lost
in the frog's scream.
    For me,
you are always man,
my eternal chimera.

RAMENDRAKUMAR ACHARYACHOWDHURY

(1922—)

Although publishing since the late forties, recognition came later to Mr Acharyachowdhury, when he won the national Sahitya Akademi Award in 1987. The prize winning collection *Brahma O Puntir Mauri*, Calcutta, 1985, is the source of the poems included in this volume. 'Water mirror' (1949) and 'Green blue yellow' (1961–62) give a sense of his lyricism; whereas 'Commotion' and 'I can't', both dating from 1975, show a movement towards the existential density of everyday life, but within a perspective of transcendence.

Commotion

Bequeath me with a fief
in one corner of the room
where I shall sleep
with my heart. Sound, sound,
such stir, endless noise.
I shall go to the forest with
a heifer and a servant girl.
As soon as the sun sets, people
come continuously — brothers,
sisters, adults all; weddings,
rites and rituals go on.
There's a surfeit of relatives,
acquaintances; pillows, rugs,
pots and pans. Nothing is
one's own.
The broken cot overnight,
in a trice, turns into common
property. Somebody's in-law
has dropped in and my fief
in the corner is taken over.
There's singing in a loud,
bass voice. This set-up is
the society of
children-friends-women.
I am on my back on the floor.
Right next door, someone pulls
a chair noisily, whistling
in unison and then laughs;
a saucer splinters. The rhythm
falters, the quick hand slips
off the straight line. Midway,
in the parchment's mirror,
in the water, as if a skiff,
a picture swivels round — my
poem. Night and day, such
keen oppression. Let's go
then to the attic.
But there, too, a winged plane
crashes into my body and I
descend the stairs. Everywhere,
a plethora of junk lying
around. Would I ever be free
anywhere?
    At midnight, there's

the passion-broken voice
of Siraj: General! General!
(crowds gather slowly around
their favourite play). This
princely crown I put at your
feet. (O god of night, on this
cursed forehead mark
your grace
in a circle of sandal paste).
A huge cannon demolishes
the castle. There's a gaping
hole in the mosquito net.
The night's lorry goes
who knows where shaking
the window panes, shattering
sleep.
I wish, for a few days,
alone, in a corner,
I could lie, a homely frog,
flat, inert, silent,
in winter's suspended
animation. But who grants me
that wish?
Is there silence anywhere?
Only great noise: pompous
speeches in the town hall;
tourists at monuments; lovers
in the boat, at the river
bank. Crowds. Crowds. Endless
heads of people (I feel terror)
on the road, in markets;
the crowds of suitors in
the drawing room of the golden
hued girl; in the hands of
poets superfluities.
Those, who, daily, steam out,
smoke out sorrow
from coloured containers,
would they allow me rest?
And you, village pond,
once by your side, you let
one watch the struggle between
the peasant and the earth
— but there too now social
commotion, secret fear in
daylight, pistols, fire!

I can't

Within the fingers' reach,
pearls,
diamonds in the trees, garden
of winged dreams. And to guard
such pearls, diamonds,
to snatch at these emeralds,
in all four directions
of the earth,
in its every corner,
there's the idolatry
of weapons;
swords, sticks, knives,
bayonets, cannons, guns
all marked with sacred
vermillion.
Both sides, variously, parrot
mantras, shaking fists waving
flags, shout —
Victory, People,
Victory, Motherland.
    And I, touching
my forehead with folded hands,
offer my prayer:
on the side of those
who starve, drift aimlessly,
live luckless in their
windowless shacks, those who
die for lack of water, little
by little, for those
who rot in dark prisons,
flash out
your weapon forged
in stars.
    To the Sound, my prayer
is only for myself.
The clock recites hymns of
praise. The sleepless night
ends. In the reddening east,
there are but a couple of
birds.

And I, with violent nails,
am tearing the heart out
of the white parchment, blue
lips moving, pent passion
steaming up . . .
    I can't articulate,
pronounce words.
From time to time,
with tremendous effort,
a harsh, piercing, broken
cry — I can't.

Water mirror

As if love were a clear mirror
                    of water.
Whatever is asymmetric, whatever
distorted,
it makes beautiful.

Just as my face,
in creation's contorted signatures,
is opaque, repulsive.
Even then I know,
one day,
for an incadescent maid,
this face
was a wondrous parade
of light and shade.
Eyes resting on eyes,
one day,
from cerulean dream
dream
had surged
in some palpitating heart.

Green blue yellow

Green, blue, ochre —
green blue yellow;
monday, tuesday, wednesday,
thursday, friday, saturday
brightly, noisily turn.
In such solitary,
meditative posture,
my dear, why do you burn?

As soon as the sun sets,
a bird on a drooping vine
from the geography
of the open page, says:
'You are no longer
what you used to be.'
Her throat is painted
in moonlight, where silver filigree
burns.
We stay in two worlds
in divergent commotions.

A girl whose hair smells of songs,
I think of her sadly,
in winter or spring.
The afternoons can bring her
no serene other shores.
Not in the waters,
not in the wind,
only the fiery vermillion
at the hair's parting.

SHAMSHER ANWAR

(1944—)

Mr Anwar teaches at a Junior High School in Shahapur, West Bengal and has published extensively. 'Futility' and 'Relentlessly' were published in *Shat dasaker Srestha Kavita* (ed. Pabitra Mukhopadhyaya), Calcutta 1976. 'The woman, the swans' comes from *Ekbacharer Sreshtha Kavita* (1974), Calcutta 1975.

Relentlessly

Earth's hell drowns in the beggars' cry
    for relief.
Everyone cries like that.
Hospitals cry insolvency; ships scream
like blind beggars; klaxons blare.

    In nightmares, the man sits
before a female body, deaf, dumb,
and blind, yet looking
for something, screams
after a moment of resting his face
in her body's pool, retreats
in fear,
caroms off
and away.
But where? Even out there,
thousand upon thousand of stars
and planets,
beggarly, crippled, soiled,
circle in meaningless, inexhaustible
emptiness.

And so it goes, round
and round.
The finger twiddles around
a finger.
The eyeball rotates. Electrons,
neutrons, protons.
And beggars circle around beggars.

Futility

Nowadays, I can't
    look people in the eye.
    I feel diffident.
Inside, a palace keeps crumbling
    all the time.
    No one hears.
A perennial cripple,
I keep listening to the neighing
    of a senile nag.
So, nowadays,
    I can't look a man
    or a woman
    in the eye.
The footprints of the fugitive deer
and the zebra
    are stamped on my forehead.
    Although innocent,
I have been sentenced for life.
    And my eyes
    are full of emptiness
    of that terrifying kind of emptiness
    which yawns
    beneath the scaffold.
This hungering, thirsting prisoner
    can't make it
    to the cool lake
    of your gaze.

The woman, the swans

An enormous dark bell
tolls
through your body,
spreading terribly cool
sounds
all around.
The resonant wind is tender.
I want to embrace
that yielding, green,
fat fruit.
Can't you offer us refuge,
like a garden's giant limbs
sheltering
beggars and idlers?
What could you lose,
if you were a pleasure garden
for us poets?
But you remain
a carefully tended
village pond
and the poet's swans
are self-absorbed
as their dark calls
fill your body
with huge and tender grace.

SUKANTA BHATTACHARYA

(1926—1947)

A lyricist of force, passionately interested in political and social issues of the times, Sukanta in his all too brief a life showed a remarkable poetic range. He was a Marxist, but his concern for what is human seems to transcend ideology. The poems in this anthology are taken from *Collected Works of Sukanta Bhattacharya*, Calcutta 1967.

O great life

O Great Life, it's no longer a matter of verse.
Let tough, severe prose prevail,
Erasing the grace of measure,
The lilt of the lyric gone stale.
Let the hammer of prose
Relentlessly ring on the anvil.
There's no need for the tenderness of poetry.
Poetry, as of now, you are on holiday.
In this reign of hunger,
The earth is full of prose.
Even the full moon seems a half-burned flat bread.

Convoy

Suddenly, leaving dust behind,
returning from the front,
a convoy went
startling the highways,
like a swarm of maddened locusts,
Its erect canons
in the van,
in the rear, food,
ammunition.
I am a student of history.
I turned away from the window.
Towards history.
And there again I saw
a mad convoy
rushing down the avenue
of ages.
In the van, smoking guns;
and in the rear, the crowd
clinging to food.
I saw men
behind the screen
of cannon smoke,
with their hereditary,
infinite
attachment to things
growing.
And they come,
from across centuries,
forests, mountains,
seas,
with scorched,
stern faces.

Graffiti

I

On wall after wall,
    as I please.
    I write down words.
I am jobless.
    So I can
indulge my whimsies.

II

Morning and afternoon,
    just standing
    aimlessly in the gutter.
Does it really enchance understanding?
    Does it really matter?

III

A while back, it struck six.
    Sun's last rays,
on brilliant facades, climax
    the spent day's
        arrogant orgies.

IV

Continuously, blares on
    the radio.
And to be troublesome
    I am ready!

V

O my dear Nippons, my dear Japs,
    did asthma stop you
from reaching India,
    perhaps?

VI

And you dear Germans, my Krauts,
    you were invincible.
But all has changed,
    since your recent routs.

VII

Alas, my princess,
    here, where crowds press,
    my advice is, to wit,
today there's no niche
    where you fit.

VIII

The wick,
    sobbing,
says to the dark:
    I am no longer
        for burning.

All too suddenly

My secret sun's about to set.
I listen to murmurs from the other side.
From some carcass lying inert,
A vulture turns its red-rimmed eyes.

Sunset's dusty skies aver
The terrible nearness of death.
Yet, on this your huge, wide earth,
Spring still lingers everywhere.

In the dense, close by cypress groves,
Silence rings the darkness.
Along this stretch of path, its gaze weaves
A language that's quite wordless.

My twilight is descending slowly.
I feel beaten by the far away.
An old rook in the banyan tree,
Endlessly, spreads anxiety.

It's evening now, evening.
I knew that death was always behind.
And now that the dark is thickening,
There's that touch of its hand.

Moment

I

A moment such as this
came once before.
It seemed wonderful to be alive.
Time's shadowy trail
led to my citadel.
Leaves seared by the chill
flew in, from nowhere.
Everything cohered
with the monsoon's onset.
The air
crackled with excitement.
There was benediction
in horizon's eyes.
I had a pact
with immortality.

Even now, those moments
blossom like pale leaves
on my life's stunted branches,
fly in
as poetry's honey bees.

A moment razes dream castles
raised by other innumerable
moments.

Stripped of roots,
I know the futility of resisting
the moment
which in a flood takes me
elsewhere.
Now I keep company with constellations.
And tomorrow, the ebbing tide
may take me to the sun's court,
straddling
black hurricanes.

II

It's useless trying
to forget this moment, which augurs
your death and mine,

which brings
this poem and, perhaps,
your curiosity.
This instant, the sun rises.
And at another, some galaxy
holds levee.
I read clear omens
in typhoons.
Many an instant goes into increasing
earth's fertility,
many into reaping.
There's that in your life,
remembered ever and ever,
and then another, unnoticed,
pervasive
through sadness.

Many instants, many lives,
fill the empty hands
of my muse, with boundless
riches.
But this fierce afternoon,
time passes
in futile attempts
to write poetry.

And may be, this very instant
someone else is ecstatic
with ceaseless inspiration,
or face to face
with the arrogant wall.
I had better remember this moment's
futility.

Today, at this moment
secret with inarticulateness,
there's no east
in the impenetrable sky.
My lonely traffic
in dreams
is ended.

Each instant offers
a different plea,
to instants
not yet come.

Sunshine melody

Here the sun, unstintingly, flings
Wine with both hands, its pungent gold.
And, drunk on that yellow wine, paddyfields
Grow into hamlets, then towns, rings on rings.

India, your lovely body wears the cover
Of sunlight. It's about you in a golden chain.
Honey, of your loveliness aren't you vain,
As the sun dries the dark forests of your hair?

Endless sunshine. The whole year round.
The hills stand mute, seared by the sun.
In endless sunlight, sunlight like poison,
We suffer together, in both body and mind.

Let's ask the world to the sun's feast.
And with open fists fling out your gold,
Where forests glitter in the distant east.
Ah, to count hours in the sun! I feel enthralled.

Pitiless steel brightens in the sun's heat,
A hint of iridiscence at its core.
Sun's vassals, in fields silent and empty,
Mumble prayers to its altar.

On highways devoid of pedestrians,
Sun's herald announces a wild gala
Of sounds, beyond the noon's monkish meditations,
Assuring us of an impending, reckless fiesta.

The sun pursues the dark, thus and thus.
Honey, do you fear the clouds as they muster?
The thunder is the ring of the sun's laughter
And the cumulus are transient. They will pass.

Today, I have invoked you sun,
For my heart beats faintly, feebler is the body.
And I am like an ancient pool, stagnant,
Waiting for reflections, from beyond the shade.

21st November, 1946

Once more
that insurmountable day,
the twentyfirst of November,
rending the corners
of horizons
with lightning,
raging in death-palsied storm.
Once more,
in fields and gardens,
in far away hamlets,
in the crowd's susurrus,
that hint
of Hasnabad,
that terrifying dream
of retaliation.
Once more,
this the twentyfirst day
of November.

Behind us,
another year. Stale, stale.
Rife with strikes,
reeling from blows,
maddened.
Stranger, after so many
victories,
we know we have lost
at last.
Now, we shall snatch away
your magic wand.
Listen stranger, listen.
Once more is our moment
of winning
in a different arena.

We are savages, wild,
and shall avenge
our futile
blood-sacrifice.
That we have sworn.
One step back,

two to the fore.
We have learned
from your stratagem.
Listen to our savage cry.
The call
comes from far,
Hyderabad, Travancore.
We wait
for that stern, single voice:
'Foreign dog,
once again it's November!'
And then, once more,
relentless strikes
and marches,
revolt sprouting
like crimson blossoms.
Once more,
when the voice calls.

We are deathless,
inexhaustible
despite futile
blood-letting.
Sworn to survival, we fear
no leeches.
We are immortal with dying,
erosionless.

Once again,
the thirteenth of February
will come,
with the holding of hands,
grinding of teeth,
with serried
readiness.
If nothing else,
we can give
our blood.
From unfurled banner
to banner,
February will come.
November
bears its intimations.

Anxious moment

Villages, cities
are broken nests
starving multitudes
press
        and congest.
Volatile seas
        flame
phosphorescent
anxious waters
        break coastward.

In bruising violence,
the dreams of avenging
are relentless.
The promises keep
        only in blind eyes.
And even now, the sea
observes its limits
        despite turbulence
and floods seep
through horizons
as hurricanes impend
in feral surprise.
        Would all of this
break upon the earth
merely to be wasted?

The tide is turning
everywhere
and the riders gallop
on the beaten paths of steel,
where daily sunrise
spells apocalypse.
And the winds veer
towards that horizon.
So I wait and wait,
through the days passing
without dreams.

Futile exodus

Death's at the door;
inundated forests,
closed roads.
It knows
this our evasion
and follows quietly
our futile
exodus.
Forests burn down
as tears dry
in their turn.
Trees lie,
uprooted,
spiting
the anonymous guile
of fleeing
forest creatures.

BUDDHADEV BOSE

(1908—1974)

A militant Modernist as poet, novelist, critic and essayist, translator and anthologist, Buddhadev Bose stood out from the very inception of the Modernist movement in the '20s. 'Hölderlin' (1962) and 'Icarus' (1964) appeared in *Marcemara Pereker Gan*, Calcutta 1966. 'One day, always' and 'My tower' come from *Ekdin; Ciradin*, Calcutta 1971. Buddhadev Bose taught Comparative Literature at Jadavpur University.

Hölderlin

Still, like a completed moon
that the astral rhythm brings gently
to our window, to cypress groves, the bench
in the park . . .
and distant . . .
Those who weep, quarrel, are fatigued,
roam through flea markets
with hunched backs,
or those who gather to conspire
in muraled palace halls,
or in the temple's wide courtyard,
cannot move him with their hates,
tempt him with pity . . .
Aloof
in farther skies, as if history
were no more than a shameless
procession
or the painted mask
of a clown . . .
Only in unwavering,
inarticulate light's radiance,
detached, free and eddyless,
the gods still remain.
As if unstoppable
after this dark of the moon,
sombre, eroded . . .
one flood-driven,
possessed
by this knowledge
on a brilliant, fullmoon night . . .
One night
erased it all . . .
all that immortal force, that sound
of his lyre
aching with grace,
all seasons,
spring-ridden bright apples,
in the unbreakable embrace
of frosty waters.

Icarus

Stainless, radiant day; the sea does not breathe;
the wind is baffled in the sun-filled sky;
so calm and serene, graceful —
as if from fulfilled summer's peak,
earth's fluent suffering
has got back its articulate form.

The naked, round sky,
the brilliant, limitless sky melts,
naked and round
in timeless horizon's
unaccounted for embrace.

Completed, ripe noon; there's no strife
in the enchanted sea
and this huge horizon is a luminous response
to all longings,
as if all achievements were a promise
of this clear blue,
as if this day, at last, the curtain shall rise
on the dark thirst in each man's eyes.

A gray iota floats in the distance.
Cargo and passengers, a wealth of expected merchandise
sail eagerly to the harbour.
The sea shows no other wound.
In the sky's shimmering light,
the equatorial day
is immaculate;
endless the gold wine.

Suddenly, a mad blow:
tearing the over-ripe womb of an instant,
a flood of dark seeds
descends in fiery line. And all this radiance,
this mature summer's secret sense
cracks open the sky
like a comet's rage,
denounces the day
at the feast
of the sun and sea . . .

Head bent, feet in the air, the futile wings
weighing him down helplessly;
in relentless acceleration
downward;
the wind's whip falling soundless . . .
'Icarus! Oh, Icarus!' —
only this a song in his ears,
until the head disappears
in the water's depths;
for a moment, the feet kick;
the fangs of molten wax
let loose memory in the follicles;
then, no more sound,
no further striving.

The sea quietens, forgets the momentary distraction;
once again the wind distends, sundrunk.
The sky regains its primal integrity.

On the ship, there's a feast,
at the port's imminence: beef-sated
passengers fill their wine cups;
some pick at pimples; some fantasize
about the night's connubial
mating.
Elsewhere, in the city, during
the half-hour break, harassed clerks
get excited over the news of the moment;
which minister was caught stealing, who got
the commander's post by greasing palms,
which wrestler will win the prize
at the coming festival.

Meanwhile,
in the cool atria, their arms
moving like waves,
the ladies fling dice,
or seem agitated
that the price of honey
has gone up by at least a half-drachma,
or
lean into a catnap.

But that very moment,
    a gouty, old poet,
exhausted by effort, beyond despair's limits,
    who had understood
    that failure alone does not deceive,
        who had strangled contumely,
    flung away futile resentments,
was lying there,
    on the unstinting whiteness
    of a coverlet
        bought with his meager earnings,
    thin and dry,
        silently aware.

One day, always

At times, the noon seems like some other noon.
A little push would open it up,
a little, a little more.
Two in the afternoon. Summer beats down
relentlessly.
The sunlight is egg-yolk. Silence pervades the sky . . .
I know the house and descend from the tram
at Park Circus.
A house with a single floor, encircled by a wall;
old moss clinging to the staircase;
leaves drifting down in the courtyard.
Softly, on tip-toes. There's a noise as of tearing paper.
Did someone breathe, whisper something?
Up in the veranda, I stand by the door.
There she is. She hasn't forgotten. She lies there
ready to receive. Her body —
a golden flood; the nipples shiver like eye-balls.

An instant trembles, in a day full of skies,
as if the curtain's about to rise, as if everything
is about to recommence, right now.
At dawn, it rains in my sleep
and there's that smell of fried cereals
in the rain.
I land in the Artist's Alley,
in a helicopter, on a book's cover.
Shadows flit on the walls of the public urinal
and the vinous odor brings out goose-pimples.
Kisses are pomegranate seeds
under the night's celophane wrap.
And my heart,
the giant pendulum of an astral clock.
I feel that her breasts standing forth, invite
inspection,
simple as a girl's.

Her body — fluent, a river; golden wavelets
rise in the follicles.
I bend down to take off the shoes and the laces,
all knotted up, keep tangling.
No matter how I pull. My frantic tries
complicate, like banyans dropping roots.
Patience is a stone in my hands.

I tell her, 'Soon, very soon now. The knife
will be out of the dirty blue jeans, my flower
will burn in your blood.'
In reply, she wrests the pillow
from under her head and flings it down —
full blown, like a sail in the wind.
A little, a little more.

What guilt, what enchantment holds me captive?
Why this conspiracy of shoe laces?
Again, why are you greedy, licentious?

Time passes. The clock's ticking bites into my heart.
On the cheeks, stubbles crop. The pants are rags.
The elephant grass pierces the skin; goats devour me.

Even now, I return at times. That door, that vigil —
as if now were some other day, tremulous.
Today shudders across the skies. And even now,
I am greedy, lust-ridden.
Concupiscence is ever restless
in every bone.

My tower

Some say that my tower is of ivory.
They are wrong.
My tower is a shack
in Behala's slums,
a forty floor hotel in San Francisco,
a proud liner
on the Atlantic.
Or a toilet in Calcutta, sweating
with the Monsoon,
where cockroaches skitter over cracked walls
and the bath tub is filmed
from a prior wash.
My tower, indeed, isn't stationary,
but mobile, many formed,
alive.
Some say, I'm the tower's sole
inhabitant. They are wrong.
I keep company:
lovely women and learned men;
many deers; sewer rats;
beggars and whores
from the stinking alleys.
At times, by some prestidigitor's trick,
red and blue lotuses bloom
on the same branch.
Sometimes, an aged vulture cranes its neck
through my window.
My tower has no limits, walls, watchmen.
I don't even know the names
of those who crowd here.
They chatter to each other,
in my hearing, guzzle my food and leave.
Some say that I am safe as a corpse
in a coffin, in my tower.
They are wrong.
At times, the wind bears the deadly virus
and plague starts.
Then my tower serves as a hospital.
I spend nights listening to the groans
of those afflicted.
At times, bombs drop

and my tower billets soldiers
with rifles.
I serve them like a flunkey.
I am terribly vulnerable, easily beaten.
A bourneless debility
is the stuff of my tower.
And yet, curiously, my tower withstands
destruction,
bombs, virus, earthquakes.
At times, soaring,
at times, level with the ground
at times, in disguise, it defects
to my enemies.
And it's sly, deceptive,
like a spy.
Like the cockroaches on the cracked wall,
it's indestructible, immortal.
Like grass under snow.
This my tower.

AMIYA CHAKRAVARTY

(1901—1981)

Amiya Chakravarty was Rabindranath Tagore's literary secretary from 1926 to 1933, on returning from Oxford. Later, he was professor of Comparative Religions and Literature at Boston University. Professor Chakravarty published extensively from poetry to essays and travelogues. Among other things, he edited *A Tagore Reader*, sponsored by the UNESCO. 'Confluence', written in the late thirties, is taken from *Adhunik Bangla Kavita* (ed. Buddhadev Bose), Calcutta 1973 (first published in 1940).

Confluence

He will bring together
the stormy wind
and that broken door
of the ruined house.
He will bring
them together.

The mad wind's gust
won't bring out
goose pimples. In the unseasonable heat,
the fields
crack with thirst,
lick with the tongue
of the cur
of pestilence.
It's flooded, even then
it rains
in a diluvial cry.
The earth and the sky
are confluent.
He will bring them together.

You and I
fight many battles,
patriotic, social,
over name and fame,
between hunger and hunger
where conclusions linger.
He will bring
together.

Life, delusions about life,
in the mute heart, dream's revolt.
He will bring together,
bring them together.

Shaded by the noon,
the mateless bird
has spread
its wings.
The pinions

    seem painted
    in so many colours.
Though lifeless,
    yet surviving.
    He will bring them
    together.

What you or I create
    in the heart
        of his creation,
what sounds as melody
    or melodyless,
    he will bring
    together.

The dust flying from the car wheels;
    those who move away,
    only those;
    hard or stricken,
    arrogant or helpless;
those who receive and those who don't,
    despite all they possess;
what can't be made explicit,
    even when it must;
    shall be brought together.
He will bring them
    together.

In spite of all, God has assumed
    the dirty broom.
Avoiding human touch, on the path
    of pilgrimage,
I am stuck in religion,
    worshipping society.
That stormy wind
    and that ruined door,
He will bring together.
    He will bring them
    together.

NIRENDRANATH CHAKRAVARTY

(1924—)

A poet, essayist, lecturer, Nirendranath Chakravarty is one of the foremost poets writing in Bengali. The poems in this anthology cover a period of some twenty years of his writing career and give some indication of his stylistic range and interests. 'Death's hand' (1951), 'On the battlefield' (1963), 'Calcutta's Jesus' (1969), although published in different volumes, are translated from *Nirendranath Chakravarty's Best Poems*, Calcutta 1970. 'Open fist' (1972) and 'Quick sands' are from *Khola Muthi*, Calcutta 1974.

Calcutta's Jesus

There was no red stop light.
Yet Calcutta, usually driven
by flurries of tempestuous activities,
suddenly came to a stop.
All taxis, private cars, double-deckers
with Tempo advertisements or Tigers
for symbols,
somehow, precariously
halted.
STOP! DO Something! They had screamed,
rushing from both sides of the street —
the coolie, the pedlar, shopkeepers and their
customers.
And even now, they are held in the stasis
of an easel, watching a naked toddler
toddle across the street.
A while ago, it had rained
at Chowringhee. And now, the sunlight,
like a long spear, reaches
through the cloud's lungs.
Calcutta is floating in a magic light.
I turn away from the sky,
press my face against the window
and watch you, beggar woman's child,
Calcutta's Jesus.
Your subtle enchantment
has brought all traffic to a halt.
You are indifferent to all;
the crowd's cry, the impatient drivers
gnashing their teeth,
death impending
on both sides.
You stumble your way between. As if at the moment
of incarnation,
in sheer pleasure of learning
how to walk, gripping
whole worlds in your fists,
you move with hesitant steps
from earth's one end
to the other.

Death's hand

Death's hand is on the pillow. The slow
movement of unspoken words gathers
as uneasy breeze.
All over the room,
the silent tangles of waiting.
In the night's huge belly, fear's flood
bloats in empty, blanched silence,
sweeps away feelings and proclivities.
There, by the door, in half-light,
a figure stands, as if in a niche,
her eyes unblinking all this time.
The moon-light falls like fatigue
by the bed. Like pity, in wordless magic.

Death's hand is on the pillow.
Nobody knows when the drawn, agonied breathing
stilled.
The window curtain shivered with the dawn wind
and then it grew quiet. Still, it's half-light
and half-dark; the rivers, forests and fields
rest in sleep.
But here, at the night's end,
he is no more. Peace. Peace.
He has gone unaccompanied, except, perhaps,
by the darkness.

On the battlefield, easily

The nights still stalk
like tigers.
Dreams still
stab sleep in the back,
titter.
I was careful.
And yet, I had left traces
behind,
here and there;
rags soaked
in gasoline,
a match.
Such things.
Memories
cling to such clues,
sniffing the wind,
come
cautiously, step by step,
stand noiselessly
by the window,
or suddenly rush
laughing,
from one darkness
to another.
And that means,
I am not
dead.
Old battles still
haunt the wind.
Nights, memories, dreams
shuffle about
on all sides;
sometimes like animals, like thieves;
or a persistent
and sly detective.
In the dark,
ambushes continue
for ever.

And that means,
I am
still
alive.
That man,
where the streets cross,
keeps me
under surveillance.
And I survive
in his animosity.
And woman, you too exist,
you exist.
So that this struggle
against innumerable enemies
may mean something.
That's why,
even now,
on this battlefield,
I can easily
blow kisses
to the wind,
in a gesture
of mockery.

Open fist

Open your fist.
Show me what's there.

Nothing.
Only what children gather
from the streets, the year round.
Nothing else.

Open your fist.
Let me see what you are hiding.

You see, only what the moody wind
sweeps from the streets.
Nothing else.
A few pebbles and sand, some dry leaves
and grass.

Quicksands

In the dark, trees
    confabulate
about who can look forward
    to this night
and who cannot.
    The wind's chill-finger
touches exactly
    that spot
where there's a river
    in the heart,
and in that river's heart
    quicksands.
And in its eddy's pull
    the sharp taloned
darkness shivers.

KAMAKHSHI CHATTOPADHYAYA

(1917–1974)

Primarily a lyric poet, Kamakhshi Chattopadhyaya began his writing career early, when in his teens. But, although an innovator in his modulation of the lyric voice and always considered among the moderns, the fragile delicacy of his poems seems to have kept him from being in the front ranks of the Modernist movement. 'Tree' comes from *Adhunik Bangla Kavita* (ed. Buddhadev Bose), Calcutta 1973.

The tree

Through the arteries of this lightning-scorched tree,
earth once blossomed, brought forth fruit,
was green or redolent.

This winter's day-end, the tree watches the far river,
where lie the burnt bones of corpses, sand
like ground bones, wheel tracks, tears of survivors.

The tree merely watches: across the river,
touching the forest top, the moon has risen,
plump like a nautch girl, dark rings under her eyes,
first pink, then white like a hospital nurse.

This tree muses:
once her body murmured with March storms,
once blue-bottles crowded her like sycophants,
once the earth touched her intimately —
today the earth has forgotten.

In the mute night's mid-sky, the moon burns
with silver flames; a few jackals furtively prowl
through the dry river bed, where burnt logs
are scattered and sand like ground bones,
and a lightning-scorched tree stands on one leg.

SAKTI CHATTOPADHYAYA

(1934—)

Sakti Chattopadhyaya brings modern verse techniques to bear on traditional, often religious and deeply personal themes to convey the sense of a culture in crisis. He is a prolific poet, with a number of volumes of poetry to his credit. 'In memory of the poet', 'Moving', 'In the temple', 'Twentythird Spring', 'That's no time for happiness' are taken from *Nirvacita Kavita*, Calcutta 1974. 'The visitor' and 'God lives in the water' appear in *Iswar Thaken Jale*, Calcutta 1975.

In the temple

In the temple, slightly below that blue spire
he lives, the begging bowl extended for
a fistful of fine rice. Everyday's beggar.

Nearby, the deodar trees form a grove.
Their thick shadows' tunnel the sky covers.
In the temple, slightly below the blue spire, he lives.

Whoever has something cheap to give . . .
gross, idealistic or base . . .
From some acre-long branch of a tree
his presents — the futile hibiscus.

Little time is wasted in his worship.
And he loves more than me
the empty fisted lake,
the bloodied mouth, the pitiful —
those not craving forgiveness.

In memory of the poet

Now you lie next to each poet.
Your yellowed hair like raw silk
spread over the tassels of the pillow.

You whisper into everyone's ear,
        come by train to vote,
your brow   your nails of stone
        strung with telegraph wire . . .
You never posted any letter in the post box
        at Saharanpur.
        You never poisoned any rats
        with arsenic.
Not once did you climb the stone horse
        at the Maidan
        and denounce China.
Now you lie next to each poet.
Your yellowed hair like raw silk
        spread over the tassels of the pillow.

That night the splashing rain
        had washed away the steps
                to the Ganges . . .
Towards dawn the banyan and the fig tree
        were brought down to earth
        with inescapable noise.
The wings of the betel nut tree
        were being stripped
        by the sudden gales . . .
        You took one breath and swam
        under the endless waters
        to the other side.
                Life's pain surrendered
        to death's aching.

That time we travelled so much together
        in the Rome of republican Julius.
        Rousseau's hunter slept by us
        in the sand dunes of the desert.
We have heard his tame lion calling
in a night without end.
        Our dreams were full of fishes
                with silver scales.

That day I understood that it was only you
        who would ride the tawny lion
                like lightning
and crack open the marble
        from earth's one end
        to the other . . .

I thought I would take you with me
        to see the Rasa festival . . .

Along the way pomegranates were in bloom.
On earth deathless love doesn't exist
        outside of bedrooms . . .
There was titanic effort behind your poetry.
Yet you threw sixes
        as if by chance.

Now you lie next to each poet.
Your yellowed hair like raw silk
        spread over the tassels of the pillow.

God lives in the water

God lives
in the water.
Someday, I shall make
an artificial lake in the garden
for him.
I live alone
and, at my wish,
god lives nearby,
in the water.

He loves
the quietus of waters.
I know it's hard for him —
this human proximity.
After all,
he isn't human.

And yet, even though he lives
in a garden of distances,
the empty space
between us
will save
our intercourse.

Moving

I'm dreadfully afraid of changing houses,
to take leave of those eternally
well-trodden back alleys.
Many certainly prefer
the main arteries;
Asphalt Road, Palm Avenue,
lit on both sides
by the newly installed neons
and the wind swimming through,
light like cotton swabs.
But I am not like the others
in such matters.
My temperament is beggarly,
from head to foot.
I wear patched up pantaloons.
And, somewhat conventionally,
I carry my boots in hand, my feet bare,
the trousers rolled up,
when crossing the Maidan
during the monsoons.

The sort you would call an original . . .
No, not quite that.
By nature, I am profoundly incapable
of borrowing, even to keep myself
in food or clothing.
And although often taken for a member
of the lumpen-proletariat,
I have my own ration card
and am not afraid to use
the honorific Mister.

Anyway, as I was saying — about houses.
I have suddenly changed residence.
And now, there's that secret wish that in this house,
I shall get it over with the task
of suicide.
The past has no pull; no emotion-charged scenes
to hold one back.
So why put off Death Unlimited?

The visitor

Miraculously, god has come
and stands
in my unpaved courtyard.
On his one side, there are heaped
Shefali blossoms
and, on the other, locked doors.
For whom he comes,
nobody knows.

He sings
and dances. Dust clings
to his wearied feet.
And yet,
everything echoes
to his dancing.
Windows fling open
on the heart's recesses.
The Shefali tree
offers its cotton.

God cries alone.
He can't understand the language of those
who trade in misery,
barter man's heritage as friends,
indifferent to victims, deploy the sand
that flood sends
for some civilisation's ends.

My lord comes and stands
in all our courtyards;
heaped blossoms on one side;
on the other, imprisoned souls and hearts.
For whom he comes,
no one quite understands.

Twentythird Spring

Twenty three years. Spring returns.
Twenty three mongrels.
Heart, my heart, are you restless
at her side glance?
Unexplored ways, here and there.
Everywhere clustering thorns.
An incarcerated Christ
this body owns.
Lips are sealed in kissing
and her face burns
under my unequivocal,
if humble stare,
in this strange land,
as luck at last turns.

For better or worse, I keep
with a firefly.
The spark at its tail
poses the question:
'Learning to swim,
but why?'

Some deluge seems ahead.
I am testing myself
against mountain peaks.
No more drifting with arms
around a brass vessel
that leaks.
A perpetual thirst
in salt waves burns.
Twenty three years. Twenty three mongrels.
Spring returns.

That's no time

Wobbling from head to foot, off walls to walls,
cornice on cornice,
the footpath changes at midnight.
Time to return home. House within the house,
foot inside foot, heart within the heart,
nothing else —
(or a lot more?).
Even before that,
from head to toe wobbly, walls within walls,
cornice on cornice,
the footpath changes at midnight.
Time to return home. House within the house,
foot inside foot, heart
within the heart,
nothing else.
'Hands up' — raise your hands — until someone
picks you up and takes you away.

Within the Black Maria, another black car
and inside that still another black sedan;
rows of windows, doors, cemeteries —
topsy-turvy skeletons;
and inside the skeletons, white maggots;
life inside the maggots, in life death —
therefore

death within death and nothing else.
'Hands up' — raise your hands — until someone
picks you up and takes you away.
Picks you up, flings you out of the car,
only into some other car,
where someone else always waits — with slaked lime
in the fist, like a banyan seedling.
Someone or other, whom you don't know, waits
like an immature bud behind the foliage,
with the spider's golden noose in hand —
and will garland you
at your nuptial midnight, when
the footpath changes
and one wobbles from head to toe,
walls on walls, cornice on cornice.

Imagine, the train left behind, the station races;
by fused electric bulbs the light of stars;
imagine shoes walking while the feet stay still —
heaven and hell at sixes and sevens;
imagine,
children hurrying to the burning grounds,
bearing the bier of the dead on their shoulders —
and on the other hand,
old men prancing their bridal dance
with long strides.
That's no time for happiness, that's no time
for joy.
Only for wobbling
from head to foot, off walls to walls,
cornice to cornice. The footpath
changes at midnight.
Time to return home. House within the house,
foot inside foot, heart within the heart,
nothing else.

DINES DAS
(1915—1976)

Dines Das' 'Sickle' ('Kaste') made an immediate stir when it first appeared in 1936. Das was a Communist and deeply commited to political and social issues. But his passion for the downtrodden and for justice, rather than dogma, lend authenticity and permanent relevance to his poems. 'Shame', 'Bengal, 1943' are both from the second edition of *The Sickle*, with a foreword by the author, Calcutta 1975. 'Sickle', which has provided the title for a volume as well as to a section of *Kavita: 1343–48 (Poems: 1936–41)*, published in 1942, in this instance is taken, along with 'Ethiopia, 1938', from *Sreshtha Kavita (Best Poems)*, 1972.

Sickle

No matter how sharp the bayonet is,
Hone your sickle, friend.
No matter how heavy the bomb and shell,
Keep your sickle honed, my friend.

The blanched silver of the curved moon,
I suppose you loved it a lot.
The time of that old moon is gone.
The sickle is our new moon, friend.

Those who had filled the world
With iron and steel —
Today, as the cannons clash,
How shattered they must feel!

The iron globe has cracked
In your sea of blood.
The earth is softened, corroded.
A new age is on the upswing, friend.

The earth, the soil is thickening
At the horizon's limits, friend.
Have you kept your sickle honed?
Of this earth, the sickle is a friend.

Ethiopia, 1938

Rainbow across Rome's skies:
the Pope's voice, grateful, prayer-laden,
'O Lord! At the diluvium's end,
You drew serenity's rainbow
across your skies,
ending all the injustice of the world.
There's no more to fear, no more.'

On this other shore,
through the wounded Ethiopian sky
flies the pennon
of that divine reassurance,
below which bodies
of men, dark as cocoa,
have turned fistfuls
of proferred flesh
at the bayonet's point;
a hundred thousand skulls shattered
by bullets.

O Lord!
And still the rainbow in your skies
and the Pope's prayers
in your Cathedral.

Shame

I am alive.
And there's no greater shame,
dishonour.
Day, night, all around
are the sounds
of lamentation;
the crowding dead and dying.
And, despite it all, I bear
this primeval body,
shamed by living.
Alive, still alive.
There's no greater shame,
dishonour.

Once, I could strangle
a tiger
in a single fist
and with the other
take the poisoned spear
to the shark's
gullet.
Then, I announced
for life,
obliterated death.
Once, on this Bay of Bengal,
I flung millennia
like handfuls of sand;
fistfuls of life, bright
like sand.
But where, where are they gone,
those jungles of Sunderban?
A child of the forest,
I roam back-alleys, begging
for food.
And I am still alive.
Nothing can approach such shame,
dishonour.

Daily, I kick aside
a hundred carrions
and go on living,
unquestioning.
I kick aside corpses
of those who had sweated
over fields,
planting seeds.
And, as I gorge down
their meagre portions,
in all seriousness,
I ask if I am
still alive.
    If I am,
there's no greater shame,
no greater dishonour.

Bengal, 1943

They come like long-drawn sighs
and are wiped off like tears.
They come and go.
Earth's green veins
turn blue;
the sea-spray
seems like tears.

They come like agony's breath
filling stony skies;
like black fog, opaque
and bending.
Sun's honed razor
cuts through them,
repeatedly.

They come like long-drawn sighs
and are wiped off like tears.
Like dew swept off grass blades.
Earth's green
hardens and sears.
But earth remains impervious
to pain.

Their hunger soughs
like gales over flood tides.
They come accompanied
by famine and plague.
Death juts out of their bones.
They come, again and again.
1776. 1943.
And they come again.

JIVANANANDA DAS

(1899–1954)

A pioneer of the Modernist movement from the era of small magazines like *Kallol* in the '20s, Das, as a literary historian put it, was almost a symbol of Modernism. Undoubtedly, his popularity and high reputation were widespread. Rich in imagery, resonating to the rhythm of common speech, his poetry seeks a definition of the lyrical self within a contemporary historical frame wherein inherited myths serve as symbols. The poems in this collection date back to the forties – 'Banalata Sen' from *Banalata Sen* (1942); 'Naked solitary hand' from *Mahaprithivi* (1944), as also 'The wild ducks' and 'The world'; 'Night', was published in a collection in 1948. All of them have been taken from Jivanananda Das' *Sreshtha Kavita*, Calcutta, 1954.

Banalata Sen

I have walked earth's byways
for millenia
from Ceylon's coast
to the archipelago of Malaya,
in the night's darkness,
moving ever.
I have been a guest
at the now hoary court
of Vimvisar
and Asoka;
in the further dark
of the city of Vidharva.
Life's seas foamed
all around. I was weary.
And my sole respite came,
when
I spent a couple of hours
with Natore's Banalata Sen.

Her hair dark, like some long gone
Vidisha's night,
her face like Sravasti's delicate
handiwork.
Like some mariner,
helm lost, gone astray
in far seas,
by chance discovering
the greenness
of Spice Islands —
I saw her in the dusk.
And raising eyes, like bird's nests,
she asked: 'Where were you
so long?'
She asked me then.
Natore's Banalata Sen.

Evening comes at all our day's end
like the sound of dew.
The kite wipes off sunshine's scent
from its wings.

When all the earth's colours are spent,
in the fireflies' brilliant hue,
completing an unfinished tale,
an old script
finds a new arrangement.
All the birds return home,
all the rivers.
All the day's transactions end.
Just darkness remains
and sitting with me
face to face,
Banalata Sen.

Naked solitary hand

Again the sky thickens
    with darkness.
The light's riddle-spinning twin sister
    is this darkness.
    A woman, her face unknown,
ever in love,
    this March sky
    is intense,
    with darkness.

The tale of an abolished city
    comes to mind, with the infatuating charm
of its palaces
    at sundown.
On the Indian ocean
or the Mediterranean,
or, may be, by the Tyrrhean sea,
    once there was a city
    and it had a palace
full of costly accoutrements:
    Persian carpets;
    cashmere shawls;
the sea-perfected pearls
    and corals;
my razed heart, my dead eyes, my evanescent
    longings;
    and you, my lady.
All of you existed once.

    And there was sunshine
of the colour of oranges;
    parrots and pigeons;
the leaves of mahogany trees
    thickening shadows.
And sunshine
    of the colour of oranges.
Sunshine like oranges.
    And you, too, were there.
I haven't seen you now
    for a hundred centuries.
Because I do not seek.

And a March evening
brings back
that tale of oltremar:
the achingly lovely lines
of arches and spires;
the lost odours
in the flaring nostrils;
the innumerable, graying manuscripts
of deer and lion skins;
rainbow coloured window panes;
and the hint of a recessional
in the swaying curtains
of the colour of peacocks;
rooms echoing farther rooms;
distances.
A momentary stasis in timeless pause
is wonder.
And there was the marginless taste
of orange sunlight
on curtains and tapestries;
and red, melon coloured wine
in the goblet,
in your naked, solitary hand.

Your naked, solitary hand.

Night

Opening a hydrant, a leper licks the water.
Or, perhaps, the hydrant was leaking.
Midnight descends on the city like a gang.
A car goes past, like an imbecile, coughing

Out volatile petrol fumes. Someone, despite
Infinite carefulness, stumbles head first
Into a drain. Three rickshaws rush past,
Disappear, by some trick, into the last gaslight.

And I, leaving Fear Lane, after mile on mile
Of rash meandering, stand here by a wall
In Bentinck Street. Near the Market.
In a breeze that's dry like a monkey nut.

The warmth of reeling lamps caresses my cheeks.
The smell of kerosene, timber, lac,
Jute, the pungent odour of hides mingle
With the murmur of dynamos, form polarities

Like a bow-string, hold the dead and living
Together, sharpen contraries.
The psalm-singing priestesses are all gone
And long gone Attila with ruined kingdoms.

From an upstairs window, in a tune quite her own,
A half-somnolent Jewish lady croons.
The dead patriarchs smile. They knew the difference
Between oil wells and the Mint, music and gold mines.

Some Anglo-Indian boys saunter past, fastidious, trim.
A fat negro, laughing, leans against a pillar,
Cleaning the Briar pipe with a finger tip.
He knows, like some aged, old gorilla

That this great city night is a jungle
And its creatures quite original — salaried —
Wearing clothes out of some secret shame.

The wild ducks

On dusky wings, the owls fly towards the stars,
Deserting the marshes at the moon's beckoning.
I listen to the swish of the wild ducks' wings —
One, two, three, countless times, as they fly afar.

Swift, full-stretched, they move towards the night's edge,
As if on engines. They hurry on and on,
Leaving a desolate sky with its cortège
Of stars. Their smell lingers in fancy's swans.

Arunima's face, from my village of long ago,
Comes to mind. Let phantasy's swans through this mute,
Moonlit November sky fly on. Let them go.
When all the earth's colours and sounds are gone,
They will sweep through again in the heart's full moon.

This earth

Far and near,
    repeatedly,
houses, cities
crumble;
    there a hamlet collapses
with a crash.
    After millenia
on this earth,
the shadows we cast
    are of fear
and death, of loss
    and bewilderment.

There's little
    but such emptiness
on time's margin.
    And yet,
cradling the sheer
    wasteland of remorse,
    of blunders,
    projects and plans,
there's another
    world,
    gentle with the whispers
    of exotic
    trees;

    this earth,
    this love, this knowing,
    this posting
    of heart's address.

VISHNU DEY

(1909–1987)

A poet of delicate lines and formal control, Vishnu Dey's poetic career began in the '30s. He taps the various sources of the Bengali literary tradition – among others, the Vaishnava lyrics. 'Paul Robeson', on the other hand, indicates his outward reach. He won the national Akademi Award in 1965. The poems in this volume are taken from *Smriti, Satta, Bhabhishyat*, Calcutta 1973. The title – Memory, Consciousness, Future – gives an idea of his major concerns. Of the poems included here, 'So long ago' and 'Futile vigil' date back to 1956 and the rest to 1958.

Birthday

The earthen lamps burn for him. The mark
on his front comes from mother's finger-tips.
A garland of Bel blossoms sway from his neck
and from his loins a new dhoti in pleats.
His older sisters give him so many gifts —
books and toys and huge, huge kisses.
After fish head and milk pudding, on this
his birthday, all life lies at his feet.
Who recalls today the luckless present?
He is a hero, time's own champion,
in such a brief life. As he smiles, old and wry
faces break into smiles of delight. I turn,
in dream's purity, to that child's birthday.

I know, on the usual anniversary,
the funereal meet's chill wind blows.
Such are our customs, temper of the country,
that, with age, fear and need deny birthdays
and, as socal props, haunt life's alleyways.
That's why one looks for an old man's undaunted,
long hoarded smiles of sheer pleasure.
That's why I match that day with childhood's promise
and invite to my domain an ageing exile.
I'll mumble to myself, watching children
smile as they play and study.
Today, in life, in death, there's no contention.
Love, with its natural auspiciousness,
as for us both, in a pristine alb,
unites now and then, time's venom cancels —
where dream is birth and death — a smile past struggles.

So long ago

It was so long ago
    when I sang your praise,
fulfilling the melody.
    Now the hymnal is erased
by monsoon rains.
    What remains
    is memory.
But neither the sun
    nor the waters
    can kill
    remembrance,
    with its longevity
    of steel;
    only
    in the soul's aching nerve,
    those grace notes
    and the verve.

As I was saying

I remember it well. The day was suave.
A hundred clouds cast blue shadows in the sun.
Among the quiet pearls of tobacco blossoms,
The stern bluebottles seemed agitated.
When all of you went off to the garden,
I didn't accompany you, lacking words.

At times, when our eyes meet, it still seems
That moment acquainted us for ever.

I remember well your glance's reassurance,
A hundred clouds casting shadows on that keen noon,
The soft spread of your fingers in that cruel time.
Yet, I didn't go to the garden with the others.
And in the dark grove of your gathered hair,
I didn't look for bluebottles, sought no lien.

I still remember. Now that you are middle aged,
One can confess, after the long play at knowing,
What I couldn't then say spontaneously.
As the sun sets, with calm pure daring,
Would you make gentle my impending night?

Paul Robeson

For us all, it's true nature's victory.
His life's fierce sun has subdued barbarous waste,
Abolished the barriers of country
And society, cancelled all their debts.

It is a kind of nature's paean to man.
His sun tinted body, with the dignity
Of an adamantine hill; in his voice,
The thunder clouds are at one with the high seas.

In nature's triumph, he has captured history
In an immaculate heart; in his red corpuscles,
His is the reassurance of the universe.
What cowardly slaves can imprison genius?

In life's radiance, versatile; his home
In all lands; the artist has filled
Our heart's horizons with dramatic aplomb.
In his freedom, man's voice resonates from the skies.

Futile vigil

Memory's futile vigil.
Futile shutting of doors.
If I open the window,
Days, nights flee to time's dark hill.

Adolescent loneliness
Aches in old bones now.
Heart's monsoon flares
Into Sahara's righteous heat.

I am in a void.
When you last came, I forget.

If someday you return . . .
I watch the Bakul saplings grow
And keep your garden.
If someday you come,
Daily I gather flowers.

NABANEETA DEV SEN

(1938—)

Born to a literary family – Mrs Dev Sen's father Naren Dev was a novelist and her mother Radharani Devi both a poet and novelist of distinction – she is a humourist, a writer of children's stories as well as a poet. Both 'The real thing' and 'One day, like Gregor Samsa' were published in *Ek Bacharer Sreshtha Kavita* (1974), Calcutta 1975. Nabaneeta Dev Sen is professor of Comparative Literature at Jadavpur University in Calcutta.

One day, like Gregor Samsa

One day, like Gregor Samsa, in the morning . . .
Look, look how your life and world
metamorphosed. Ah,
did you ever think that this may happen,
would happen!
Did you ever think that so easily,
effortlessly, life-long bonds would fall away!

Now look, how light are the hands and feet,
the ribs have melted and are cotton soft,
the muscles are like thin, thin paper,
can be torn.
    Now if you stab me,
not a drop of blood would spill.

In the afternoon, the part-time maid will sweep
the dead insect
into the garbage bin.

The real thing

Somehow, one didn't get to know
the real thing.
I have learned this and that,
this or that way, sense, nonsense,
backward
or forward.
But somehow, one didn't get to know
the real thing.

Months and years
have passed, just getting to know
the intricacies
of things.
And now, youth is at low tide;
hair gray; teeth loose;
goose pimples invade the body
at the thought.
Only somehow, one didn't get to know
the real thing.

I can't be shameless. But,
if not hurried,
I can make love.
Grammar's under control; the Primer
mastered way back.
I have even learned how to dive
into the blue sea.
And I can even draw water in a bucket
from the well.
There's hardly anything to learn.
A roofer, I can put a roof
over my own head.
I can act the priest and offer worship
to the deity.
As my own mid-wife, I can deliver
my own offspring.
Only how to bury my own dead body
remains unlearned.

Somehow, one didn't get to learn
the real thing.

AJIT DUTTA

(1907–1984)

Although a pioneer of Modernism, along with Buddhadev Bose (his first volume of poetry *Kusumer Mas* appeared in 1930), Ajit Dutta eschewed militancy. His themes are often traditional, his sensibility romantic, relatively free of either intellectualism or ideology. 'Where silvery' and 'Or else' both appeared in *Adhunik Bangla Kavita* (ed. Buddhadev Bose), Calcutta 1973.

Where silvery

Where on argent waves, the peacock ship sways
And the prince has seen the maid in his dream;
Where a pink princess, alone at her windows,
Spreads out her hair. With distance her dark eyes brim.

Petrified city. There even an eye lash
Won't, at all, tremble in age after age,
And jewelled flowers, fruits in gold gardens flash.
If ever, for me, to such a land you voyage,

Then I tell you. There's a lady with dice,
Who wins as wagers the lives of all men.
Ask that enchantress of such loveliness,
Of my name, ask her for my address then.
Go carefully, lest your eyes drink her magic,
Lest you hear her low voice sing sylvan music.

Or else

Do you know
    any tricks
of wrestling?
    Can you keep on
hanging coolly?
    Or else,
    you won't
        ride on
    tramways —
        standing,
    non-plussed,
down on highways.

Have you, at least,
    practised
sprinting,
    leaping, plunging,
dashing pell-mell?
    Or else,
    stay at home,
    lest
    you get
        run down
    by a car,
    or a lorry.

Have you teeth
    that are strong
and ready?
    And the habit
of munching
    stones?
    Or else,
    you won't
        eat any
    rice.
    For rice and pebbles
    are half
    and half.

Can you hold
    your mind
and feet
    still
    for half a day
    or so?
    Or else
    you won't
buy any
    clothes,
    even if
you beg
    at the shop.

MRINAL DUTTA

(1940—)

Mr Dutta has published poetry in various magazines and is the editor of the literary review *Satabhisha*. 'Letter from the countryside' appeared in 1987.

The dark countryside

The letter comes, off and on,
as if suddenly
flying in
from another planet, from some
enchanted land.
Most mysterious and secret
is the letter. It flies in
through autumn clouds,
like a sere leaf.
The letter comes
from some tremorless, windless
countryside.
There's never
any postmark on it. Yet, I sense
clinging, in the discoloured ink
on the blue envelope,
the immaculate bright fuzz
of heather,
dew drops.
Someone has written the letter,
some one from Chaitanyapur
of the dark countryside,
from the postal district
of Mathrun.
With great furtiveness,
an insubstantial postman drops
the phantom letter
into the post box.
Someone I have never seen.

In the letter,
there are rows on rows
of indistinct alphabet,
code language,
I can't decipher.
But in the blurred lines,
I can see the picture of a
countryside, broken by looming,
isolate, viscous darkness.
Like a still-life, slightly
discoloured, fragmented,

almost erased,
the end of a feudal era.
I can see a panoply
of emblems
and their worn out altar, palatial
ruins full of mute lament.
From the empty, hollow interiors,
as if someone beckons,
in green sign language,
someone else, come
to the darkened countryside.

SUDHINDRANATH DUTTA

(1901–1960)

Although he started writing poetry in his teens, it was with the publication of *Orchestra* (1935) that his reputation as a poet was established. A translator, an essayist with an interest in philosophy, a critic and theorist of literature, he was perceived as Tagore's successor by many. His poetry avoids colloquialism and slang in favour of high diction, prefers formal decorum to free verse conventions. Dutta was professor of Comparative Literature at Jadavpur University. 'Ending' and 'Waste' formed part of *Orchestra* (1935), 'Hell' of *Krandasi* (1937) and 'Doubt' of *Uttarfalguni* (1940).

Waste

Remember, my love, that first loquacious night,
The bacchic ululations of the crowd,
The flute's savage lament, the drum — ecstatic, proud,
And footfalls in heart's darkness, tentative, light?

Remember, that fierce, frenzied festival,
The drenched palms, the naked surprise as our eyes met?
We were pilgrims on an empty road and set
Shame aside, entangling oaths, fears which were mutual.

That innocence is gone in futile acrimony
And by blind touch tamed that dreamy embrace.
It was will-o'the-wisp, not morning star — your face.
Our passions drown in the waves of a shoreless sea.

Yet, hope lingers. On this stricken earth, it can't be
That such waste would be allowed by destiny.

Hell

In the dark, there's no east or west.

The elongate night,
like a whore
bloated with age,
alone on a difficult pilgrimage,
has fallen asleep
by undying habit
by the hospitable side
of the unknown.
Her rags, full of rents, poison
the air
in this narrow hovel; her head,
full of lice, lolls
on my shoulder, an outflung arm
clings round my neck.
Time and again, the anxious quake
of her hidden nightmare
ripples
through the racial memories
of my unconscious.

Sleepless eyes
see nothing.
Only my diffident body
senses gathering nameless shapes
at the head of the bed.
They come in herds, from some museum,
ghosts of extinct fauna,
alien, appalling,
to destroy inchoate longing
and disembodied shame,
discontent, futile resentment,
and all this my impossible,
unfulfilled pride
and confabulate where they hide.
In the steep, impervious Hades
of forgetfulness, carrions of spent luxuria,
of fleeting enjoyment,
defeat the sterile present
and water the unflowering seed.

Lady, where are you,
in this night's obese body?
Look into my face,
with your unfathomable, dark,
unincarnate eyes,
brimming
with a star's cold brightness.
Let fall your untouchable, fine,
incomparable tresses
over your cerulean, alien skies,
in reassurance
lucid as a dream, like Berenice,
at the moment
of self-sacrifice.
To the accompaniment of the autumnal breeze,
call to my disembodied soul
on this night bed,
across the near uncrossable
chasm of denial.
What Nachiketa saw, unperturbed,
head bent down, poised
at the angle of detachment, extinction —
the radiant, golden body
of naked earth,
swimming in foaming seas,
at the end of night's orgies;
for his temptation,
displaying all her wares of youth,
charm and grace, colours, perfume,
like a woman on a tryst
plangent with lust —
there, there summon me,
O unincarnate.

Futile. There's no response.
In a prison of emptiness,
secret inhibitions surround my urgent plea.
In this impenetrable dark, more I try to flee,
more I run into its wall,
fall in a bloody mire,
where corpses
of those who were born before

roll
in the stench of worms.
There voracious saurians, fat
with lassitude,
creep through mounds of carrions
and refuse,
and coiling serpents crawl
after sweat.
Rampant there are slimy toads,
thieving rats,
sharp taloned owls
and dark winged bats.

My soulless body, vomit drenched,
lies in hell's miasma,
in a quietus
of quenched light,
pecked at by the night's vultures
at their will.
Inescapable. Inescapable. I know.
I am sentenced to bear
what can't be borne.
And therefore, self-defence
is absurd
and all resolves are empty boasts.
Life's thrust
is to make one submit —
to the vampire's lust.
To make us endure
with detached passivity
the carrion's company and the carrion eater's
proximity.
Her magnificent incarnation
is possible only in dreams.
We wake alone.
And that festive thread of love
around the wrist
is no more auspicious
than a viper's coil.
Ecstacy can soil,
as it weaves webs
for the careless fly.

My private hell
has spread,
breaking all bounds
in a world without bournes,
as infected worms from the dead
now reign in all
our bones.
Time's tide ebbs
and feet slip in the slime.
There's no escape,
no escape from these webs.
Life's only truth
is pain.
And if it were not,
this pilgrimage would halt,
again and again.

All around is an infinity,
landscaped in darkness;
where everything is nightmare
and even you are an incubus.

Doubt

No, by no means is she ugly.
Her face glows with a kind of charm.
And if one can't call her beautiful,
Peace seems poised in her palm.

The twin plaits on her back are no dancing snakes;
And bluebottles aren't envious when she brushes her hair;
Yet, if a curl, with the breeze, on her forehead shakes,
I am grateful to the gods that she's there.

Her black, restless eyes don't really burn;
Nor, like the morning star, suggest what's infinite.
Still her glance can set beauty's margin
And words gain body by her wit.

Her voice, like Krishna's flute, doesn't call
when I am lonely;
She's no midnight visitor in my phantasies.
But non-sequiturs on her lips, and on her lips only,
Are deeper than Vedic profundities.

One can't compare her playful smile
To some dawn-reddened stream.
But when someone drops in, her startled pleasure
Seems the completion of a dream.

Her tears are no string of pearls
I have seen, nor does incense shadow her.
Yet, if hurt or rejected, in quarrels,
Her whole body seems quick with thunder.

Her breasts are no snowy peaks
Which exile flowers, as a poet would say.
The saree around her body's unnamed slopes
In clean fold spirals its way.

I haven't noted any stairs of Eros
Sculpted by flesh at her narrow waist.
But, as she goes about her chores in the house,
My love tautens with her haste.

She's no swan with love-lorn, thrusting bosom,
As the black rain clouds boil and seethe.
And yet, from the angles of her slight form,
From time to time, something sensual would breathe.

No one would say she's a river, laden with pollen,
Rushing from its source to a tryst;
That forming arches to an attained Eden,
Her thighs taper like plantain fruit.

No, let imagination stop there, still
Triumphant — and ask pardon in defeat.
Do I then love her against my will?
And is it doubt that palpitates as heart beat?

Ending

Is all forgotten, then?
That promise
in the distracted ecstacy
of impending
separation.
And not a word saved
from time's grasp.
Not one word,
now that spring is gone.

Do you remember,
at the parting of ways,
that final,
unending kiss,
when you willed to possess
my isolate soul,
in a savage, autumnal night?
In your mute eyes' intensity,
an unbearable plea
relented the breathless
pace
of that incomplete
instant.
And in a voice, small and tight
with arrogance,
you had defied
all partings:
'I shall not forget.'

If this marauding, barbaric spring,
in your undefended heart,
has turned that old tale
upside down
and you own
to a sweeping lust
in the drunken, restless scent
of the barely opened lilacs,
that seeks out
invisible pores and comes rushing
into your stricken graveyard;
if in the night's depth,

the devious breeze
brings anarchy's harsh invitation
to tamed instinct;
and your futile heart
borne down
by absconded passion,
falls at the first
ravisher's feet;
let all be fulfilled
as it must.
Let not your bounty,
in false devotion,
grow venomous.
Let not body lose its rites
and turn upon itself
in the scorpion's bitter sting.

I have renounced ownership,
inane curses, crippled jealousy,
the lapsed liens
on your imagined face.
My longing for your unreachable body
won't endure,
age after age,
like some decaying vampire's.
Forget it all and cast out
of your soul
the burrowing roots
of dead promises.
Let the lapse
of a tired incubus slip off
your awakened self,
like a worn dress
set aside on a lover's return.

Only,
some spring time at twilight,
when you sit
on the river bank, with a new friend,
your eyes inexplicably wet,
your body prone
with the intoxication of lassitude,
and watch the night lighting

its candles of stars
with the last spark of the day;
remember, if you will,
that another spring, on a night fall
such as this,
here by this wooden bench,
another pilgrim
sat at your feet and woke you
with his gratuitous words
on another shore.
But if that remembrance brings any shame,
forget it all,
even his name.
And all shall be, as it must,
received by a willing heart.

SUNIL GANGOPADHYAYA

(1934—)

Sunil Gangopadhyaya writes prose fiction as well as poetry, although his reputation was first established as a lyric poet. His poems in this collection are taken from *Nirvacita Kavita*, Calcutta 1974.

Ice age

From body's battlefield
    I run to far distances
        before returning to my body.
You promised to teach me
    passionless coupling.
    You have washed your breasts
    with dew,
    gentle like moonlight
    your body's opening.
    Like honeyswept grass
    the hair,
        russet.
    You promised to teach me
        passionless coupling.

    Breathing
    is hectic. I sweat
    too much. My mouth too full
    of praise.
        You promised to teach me . . .

Not cruel war, bloodied lips,
    lungs bursting,
    not love . . .
    love deserts after a month
    or so.
    Or perhaps a year, an age.
And even then times remain
    barbarous . . .
    You are deep as a river's womb.
    Cool. Angelic.
    You promised to teach me
    passionless coupling.

I wake next to a dead city
    and find plague.
    Atoms disintegrate
    into nothing.
    If a dream is disagreeable,
    there are ways
    to review.

Man lives, man dies
in false dreams . . .
your breasts
washed with dew,
gentle like moonlight
your body's opening . . .
you promised . . .

Now I am before you.
Desolate. On my knees.
Keep your word.
Not stallions in the blood,
teeth marking breasts,
tiger's clawing
and thighs astir . . .
Don't swivel your hips
as if transcending.
You are not the poetics
of heart or body.
Not even a prostitute.
The last time
you wanted to free
the earth . . .
free . . .
ice age . . .

you promised to teach me
passionless coupling.

Only for poetry

Only for poetry, this incarnation;
only for poetry's sake,
this intermittent play;
only for poetry,
I traverse the world
on a chilly evening.
Only for poetry's sake,
the unflickering grace
and the lambent gentleness
of your face;
only for poetry, are you a woman.
Only for poetry, blood is shed
and the precipitant clouds
swell the Ganges.
Only for poetry, is survival
a lure,
through the days
of resentment.
Only for poetry's sake,
I sneer at immortality.

My lord king

My lord king, I am in your retinue,
your page.
Don't you remember,
how stumbling along your heart's way,
I carried your burdens
in the moonlight,
suffered your music's goad?
Hands down,
feet in the air, how reckless
was my dancing?
Don't you remember, don't you,
in the moonlight, my king?

I have fished
in your tears.
Flesh or fowl, always alone
in bed.
And yet, somehow, I'm still kicking.
My near, dear cousin,
there's no need for whimpering.
Thanks to your love,
my mind is a bird's nest.
Let's not, dear sire, push it all any
further.
On your cheeks, I'm planting
a rose bush.
Life churns in tornadoes
and you are my storm lantern, my king.
There's no need, absolutely,
for weeping.

You presume to be all in all.
You scold or beat me, at will.
Your proffered gifts are fists
full of air.
I bring your morning's tea in bed
and it's you I am pinching.

Eyes fall away
from eyes.
I tickle your belly
as you swallow stale spittle
and then,
I lick your blood, my king.
Tum-ti, tum-ti, tum,
frenzied sticks
on the snare drum,
are reckless, restless.
Remember.

Suddenly for Neera

I saw you for just three minutes
at the bus stop.
But last night, I dreamed of you
a long time.
I saw you rigid like a knife
in the sand,
directionless;
and your body, a place for pilgrimage.
I saw you lashed by gales,
in that blue, inauspicious time
of the waking dream.
Did you go south, to the sea?
All alone?
When did you get back? Today?
Soundless, waveless,
dream's seas terrify.
You were about to commit suicide,
in just three days;
the horizons flung out
like a lost ring,
your thighs sinking
into blue waters.
You seemed a gangster's
murdered Moll.
Alone in that cloying dream,
all alone.
Now, I won't sleep for a whole year,
rather than wipe off sweat
after each nightmare.
Forgetfulness is welcome. Like a shameless
body, hiding under clothes,
I shall stay awake a whole year,
dreamless,
and visit your body, as if
it were one of those fifty two shrines,
and earn sanctity.
Your smiling face, at the bus window,
'So long, for now. Come and see us.
Soon.'
The shrill sun drowned the voices.
'Oh, stay,' or 'Let's sit there

on the Library lawn,' someone,
inside, was whispering.
And then, suddenly looking up,
the forgotten clock.
And I jumped and raced
across the street, past buses,
trams, rickshaws, crowds,
somersaulting
like an orang-outang,
barely making it
to the office lift . . .
Only three minutes
at the bus stop. And yet,
I dreamed of you so long, last night.

SANKHA GHOSH

(1932—)

Sankha Ghosh has also been a professor at Jadavpur University, like many others in this volume. He is a critic of standing as well as a poet. 'Holiday' and 'Restoration' have been taken from *Adhunik Bangla Kavita*, 5th edition (enlarged), reprinted in 1980. 'Munya' and 'My aunt Ranga' are from *Sreshtha Kavita*, Calcutta 1970.

Holiday

Perhaps it came. But I
didn't see it.
Has it now receded far away?
I shall go, go, go.

Everything, of course, is ready.
Now only leave taking,
eyes on everyone,
pranam, pranam at departing.

What name?
I have no name.
Only a couple of boats
at their moorings.
In the distance, everyone
is casting nets
into the sea.

Holiday, lord, holiday.

Restoration

Whatever was around me
Grass/rocks
Reptiles
Ruined temple
Whatever was around me
Exile
A child's primer
Lonely sunset
Whatever was around me
Destruction
Spears/arrows
Hearth and home
All altogether
Convulse
Westward
As if memory
Were a long moving
Caravan
Broken boxes
Remain in the shade
Of the mango tree
From one step
To another
Suddenly
All refugeless

Whatever is around me —
Shealdah
The full noon
Tattooed walls
Whatever is around me —
Blind alleys
Slogans
Monuments
Whatever is around me —
The bed of thorns
Lamp post
The reddened Ganges
All altogether
Encircle
The marrow's

Darkness
In their midst
A xylophone
Resonates
The Howrah bridge holds high
An emptiness
At its crown
Underfoot
Swift currents slide

Whatever around me   rivulet
Windblown hair
Naked path
Tempestuous flambeaux
Whatever around me   transparent
Dawn sounds
Body after bathing
Siva as lord
Of cremation grounds
Whatever around me   death
Each single day
A thousand days
Birthday

All altogether
Return
To memory's hands
Beggar waiting
By the wayside
In dim light
Whatever
Was   is
Two rocks clashing
Making
Incandescent
The restoration
Of so many
Days

My Aunt Ranga

Home, hearth, courtyard,
everything surreptitiously
abandoning, my aunt,
her feet still
wet, crossing
the bridge
to the canal's other side —

a scattered feather,
no one knows.

Munya

Munya — caged up all day.
Late at midnight,
quietly, quietly, I
incited her:
'Fly away. Fly
away.'
And she raised a foot
towards my chest.
It seemed a tiger's paw
in the moonlight.

SAMSUL HAQUE

(1938—)

Mr Haque lives in Kakdwip, West Bengal, in the country, and his poetry conveys a sense of deep roots. Mr Haque has published several volumes of poetry – *Hridayer Gandha, Protoplasm, Diary* among them. 'Into the newborn's hands', which appears in *Nibhanta Mombaatir Jalay Shaada Ghoda*, has been translated from *Shat Dasaker Sreshtha Kavita* Calcutta 1976.

Into the newborn's hands

Slow gathering loess
of ancestral sighs
congealed
into this prairie . . .

Blood, dripping from feet
pierced by the thorns
of happiness,
froze into this path
through the prairie . . .

From the seeds
flown on the beaks
of the bird of sorrow,
this parsimmon tree
by the pathway . . .

And this hot noon,
we have tied
a heart-shaped pot
to the date tree.

Drop by drop, its juice
will congeal into toddy
in this fierce
sunlight.

And, at the mid-point
of the moonless night,
we shall put a beaker of wine
into the new born's fist
and a trident
keen as life.

KABIRUL ISLAM

(1934—)

A subtle poet of nuances, whose easy conversational tone and rhythmic flexibility speak of great control, Kabirul Islam has published several volumes of poetry – *Kusal Sambad, Bikalpa Batas, Biday Konnagar*, to mention a few. 'You are sunward' was published in a volume of the same title: *Tumi Roddurer Dike*. For this volume, I have taken 'You are sunward' and 'Sometimes hot' from *Shat Dasaker Srestha Kavita*, Calcutta 1976, and Words within words' from *Ek Bacharer Sreshtha Kavita* (1974), Calcutta 1975.

You are sunward

You are growing too distant, nowadays.
The entire day you wear the armour
of being busy.
From behind the neck-breaking, unscalable
battlement of being busy,
are you ready for war?
Totally ready?
God forbid! I know nothing
about it at all.
I don't like this sort of warring.
Both sides preparing for parity
and then games . . .
You are so busy,
I don't get any of your news nowadays.

Is it true that you'd be pleased if I were defeated?
Well, let it be so. I shall lose the battle.
Unarmed, I shall resist you a little while,
find out how you use power . . .
how far you would go.

Unhappiness or happiness, hatred,
affection, love
or separation . . .
nothing is beyond conflict nowadays.
Were they ever?
Even then I don't like this sort
of warring.
You must break out of your armour
of being busy
and be
natural.
One must somehow break out of the
seedcover
sunward.

Sometimes, hot

Sometimes, searing, fated drought.
Sorrowing for a drop of water.
Sometimes diluvium, chaos.
Sorrowing for a fistful of straw.

Sometimes, eyes flooded.
Contending for a piece of bread.
In the fields, indeed, sweat and blood.
Contending for a span of land.

Words within words

A lot of unintentional offences
    remain unredeemed.
Of course, there's no bias
    on account of birth.
Nor is it a lapse
    of attention.
Just mere talk
    and the words,
    within the words,
    couldn't be
    conveyed.
    Just that the door,
    deep within,
    didn't open;

    neither through mere sound
    nor some magical
    invocation.

BINAY MAZUMDAR

(1934—)

Binay Mazumdar's poetry combines sensuality with intellectual complexity and projects a sense of aesthetic refinement. Both '8 March, 1960' and '16 June, 1961' appear in *Feere Eso, Caka*, Calcutta 1970.

8th March, 1960

A brilliant fish, after one flying leap,
in visually blue, but really transparent
water, resubmerged.
At such serene sight, the fruit reddened
with the thick juice of aching.

Endangered, the duck flies, fleeing ceaselessly.
For everyone knows that beneath
its white down, lie eager, warm flesh
and fat;
exhausted, it rests momentarily,
on hill after hill;
the entire marsh song evaporates and yet,
at such a time, o sea-fish, you . . . you

Or, look, tentatively, sick trees stir
the earth-wide, foliate forests
with long-drawn tired sighs;
and yet, all trees, arbours, in separate places,
for ever dream of union's breathless talk.

16th June, 1961

One had forgotten everything, coming
to the icon in flesh.
You had made all gentle, like intoxication
washing away the wounds of countless battles.
At hope's end, such was my enterprise,
to put aside the rod and reel
and go for the fishnet.
A stranger, welcome, like a foreign picture
or an unacquainted constellation,
one then feels eager for talk. And yet, a letter

gone astray, I came to the wrong address.
Fatigue sets in. As with some kite, high up,
looking for its prey, without beating its wings.
Because in some distant age, you had an assassin
for enemy, you live like a rose encircled
by thorns. And I, like a letter gone astray,
have come to the wrong address.

PREMENDRA MITRA

(1904–1988)

By the time Premen Mitra's long poetic career ended with his death, he was nearly blind and fragile, but still the master of familiar speech and easy conversational rhythm as in his poems. From *Prathama* (1930) on, his humanism is apparent in his verse. His was not the romance of the ego, but the Whitmanesque affirmation of the world. All three of his poems in this anthology come from *Sagar Theke Fera*, Calcutta 1954. Premen Mitra won both the Rabindra Prize and the Sahitya Akademi Prize.

George Bernard Shaw

History is idiotic,
    circling in its self-made maze.
At every century's end,
    sun's hot remorse
rings in dry thunder.
    No, not thunder. The honed
point of fiery language.
    His smile, ruthless, brilliant,
abjures forgiveness.

    Again and again,
you fetched fire
    to blind earth's snake-pits.
    I greet you,
    sunflare
        of lucid whiteness.

Discovery

I discover again and again
a dead continent.
Its rivers, bournes and mountains,
how often have set up the play
on life's chess board
and, in the end,
checkmated
by some incalculable move, accepted
the punishment
of premature extinction.

Sailor, companionless, alone,
you return
to cast anchor at death's harbour,
where skeletons of boats are scattered,
row on row,
daring, beyond hope.

Wherever I look, lifeless,
harsh is the earth, mute.
From above, sleeping skies
cast, from time to time,
attenuated sighs.

Dead is that great land.
I think again
of planting the seed of recurrence.

Give me ambrosia, affection,
O earth, hard and inert.
In your womb, I keep a new promise,
which will shunt aside the detritus
of ruin
and stage a fearless carnival,
begin a new game, with stakes
which were lost.

For you, a letter

I've heard you found
privacy's inaccessible castle,
a peaceful solitude —
with murmuring pines tremulous,
clinging to the lap of serried hills,
where sudden emptiness
spreads out, by the zig-zag
ascent of a trail.

The days there are distracted by distances,
the nights luxuriate with stars.

If you summon me, I may go,
vaulting the difficult moat
and sitting on the last tower's
final step,
for once savour
the taste of your contentment.

Only there's this fear.
What if your favourite star
and mine are different
and call us by different names.

Both you and I have known many dreams
sunk in quicksands.
Our plans and strategems
went down at the same harbour.
Yet, how could I take my leave?
I ferry back and forth.

Such crowds, swarms, by hunger, fear, blindness
driven,
such round, directionless, dust-smoke-deafened
sky.
Riven heart, even then, can faith make me all
tolerate?
Delirious raving this — it too will be resolved
in lucidity.

SARAT MUKHOPADHYAYA

(1931—)

A poet respected by other poets for his wit and originality, Sarat Mukhopadhyaya is not widely known, but deserves greater attention. 'The lady won't ever' comes from *Adhunik Bangla Kavita* (ed. Buddhadev Bose), Calcutta 1980.

The lady won't ever

The lady won't ever open her window,
that is to say, eyes;
in case she chances on something,
even lovelier
than herself,
that is, Beautiful.
And, the one that's Beautiful
stands nearby, grinning,
under a tree.
It's known
that he won't tap on the window-pane,
he won't knock on the door,
he will straight away
enter the room.
After that, the lady
and Mr. Beautiful will live together
for a while. A while.

SUBHAS MUKHOPADHYAYA

(1920—)

Subhas Mukhopadhyaya's poems can be lyrical but, at times, also satirical and political. The poems included here are found in *Adhunik Bangla Kavita* (ed. Buddhadev Bose), Calcutta 1973.

Proposal

Master, if you say, there's this war with such a king,
I won't demur; but pick up the bow and arrow.
So long jobless, about death I don't care a thing.
If body resists, there's your whip to my sorrow.

No roof over our heads, we have the open sky
Inside and out. The world's illusory, you've taught.
So I have taken the mantra of the hungry
And lack greed. In your barn, you are your own harvest.

O merchant! the soldier, the guard are all your own.
Please, then, please stop talking of humanity.
After that, master, god's grace being without bourne,
Shackle us with taboos, democratically.

Without weapons so far, we put on charades.
We were used to bows and arrows in our childhood.
If the enemies, suddenly, start cannonades,
We shall say, let civilised values be preserved.

We'll then shut our eyes and turn our ears to hear
some blackbird.

No matter how far

No matter how far
        I go,
threaded through a garland
        of waves,
a river's name
        keeps me company.

No matter how far I go.

        With my eyelashes
remain commingled
the serried footprints
        of Lakhshmi,
        in her tended
        courtyard.
No matter how far I go.

My task

I want the words
    to row upon the shore.
I want each shadow
    to open its eyes.
A still picture,
    I want it to move.

That any one calls me a poet,
    I don't want it.
Shoulder to shoulder,
    may I keep walking
to my life's last day.
    That I may put
my pen down,
    next to a tractor
    and say —
    This is my time off,
    brother,
    give me a bit of light.

VIJAYA MUKHOPADHYAYA

(1937—)

Vijaya Mukhopadhyaya speaks for an inviolable, if isolated, feminine identity in lyric tension with social constraints. She has been published in various magazines and anthologised. Her book of poetry is titled *Amar Prabhur Janya*. Her poems in this volume come from *Shat Dasaker Sreshtha Kavita*, Calcutta 1976.

That empty space

That vacant space, let's say empty.
No matter the lovely Dacca saree
    covering you
        from head to foot.
    No matter how you spray perfume
    as the evening comes.
There's always something
    missing.
    And you go looking
        for the salt cellar.
    And the spruced up gentlemen,
        your spruced up gentleman
        is off
        to his playgrounds.
That vacant space. Empty, let's say.
    The goldsmith drops in
        to suggest a new earring.
        Never.
        Keep the body empty.
        To float with the wind.
        As a plaything
        for dancing birds.
    The road is open;
        everywhere roads are open.
    And one day, it will come
        in royal progress,
    dominating the highways.

Irrelevant

Rain, rain. Swirling winds.
Thunder. Lightning.
Late afternoon. The fields are empty
of people
and the adjacent
burning grounds.
There's no sign of fire there.
None.
Only a bamboo hut, with wooden doors.
Doors opening
and shutting with the wind,
banging.
Again and again.
A corpse is laid out in the room — covered
in a white wrapper
from head to foot.
Even then I know
that she is a woman.
Slight, wasted body. Near the door's edge,
her feet stick up
under the cover.
Eyes closed, I saw
something of the sort.
I have seen incinerators
but never the village burning grounds.
And yet today, I saw
amidst familiar surroundings
the eerie, empty
burning grounds —
far, far
from all habitations.
A room. A dead body. The wooden door
in front. Doors, doors
shutting, opening . . . Cyclonic winds.
For days, the incessant
banging of doors.
I wanted to know
whose corpse it was
No one said anything.
There's no one to answer.
Once, I thought it belonged

to someone very close.
Then again I thought
  that it was Kadambini's
in that story.
  She had to prove by dying
that she had been alive.
I couldn't see her face
but wanted to know her.
  I shall go see mother tomorrow.
And when I ask, 'How are you, mother?',
  from her sick bed she would
whisper back, 'As you see, no change.
How are you, darling — do you sleep better
nowadays?'
After a moment's pause,
I shall nod yes.

Company

What we live with isn't love
    but anxiety.
    Love comes like an occasional guest,
entering with a smile,
    disappearing suddenly,
        with remembrances
    scattered about the house.
        And all this time,
    someone
        and anxiety,
        one of us
        and anxiety,
    we keep house,
        night till day,
    day till night.

When I die

When I'm dead, love too will die
and earth will be free,
like an emancipated whore
or a stubborn misogynist.

So much fuss over motherhood!
Even lovemaking is fraught with terror.
So much fuss over love
and over everything its tainted air.

Love moves on all fours
through towns, villages, fields and alleys.
It sits and walks, settles down, congeals.
Earth's exhausted. I have looked
into her eyes these many days.
I shall die, taking love with me.
And my parting benediction will be,
'Earth, at last, be free.'

MANINDRANATH ROY

(1917—)

Roy's sonnets in this volume show his mastery of image and metaphor as well as lyrical power. They are from 'New Sonnets' (selections from *Eka Cakhshu*, 1942) and form part of *Sreshtha Kavita*, Calcutta 1970.

Sonnet 1

Sunset's harbour, silent the trader's mast,
passive; an end to the give and take.
The ship of evening is a vampire's nest.

The parasitic gambler's dice have lost
magic, by fortune's turn or some such quirk.
In a self-made maze reason's fog is cast.

At the street's end, the beckoning light is spent;
and towers seem paralysed in quickened fear.
Catastrophe impends. The wheel runs its bent.

The past seems bright, but like an antique coin.
Prayers are idle, idle the flags at anchor.
And the port swarms with rebellious men.

In seething darkness, rings a silent laughter,
as the wheel turns to some disastrous after.

Sonnet 2

I shall never be a thorn in your way, love.
Again and again, for this I shall pray.
In an abyss of hate will lie my grave.

I am haunted by my body's carrion,
with lust's arrows. There's no news of your way
beyond bournes of senses, where you are gone.

Body's wild horses I try to hold in rein.
Take me, my love, in your world of use, I pray.
Empty flesh can't bring flowers to life again.

And what I called mine is now on display
at love's urgent, immediate auction.
And life's running steps stir the end of day.

And this body to your keeping hands I give.
In an abyss of hate shall lie my grave.

TUSHAR ROY
(1938–1977)

Tushar Roy's tragic and untimely death stilled a voice which, if strident at times, was original and distinct. His 'bilingual' poetry is thoroughly contemporary and hews close to spoken language and its rhythm. All his poems here have been translated from *Bandmaster*, Calcutta 1975.

Bandmaster

I can do maths, magic,
    hide chalk and duster.
For I am a tempestuous trumpeter,
    a Bandmaster.

The programme hadn't begun, a cabaret
    dancer, called Sarah Temple,
was just then sitting in a corner
    of the dais . . .

As soon as I touch the drum with the sticks,
    her body undulates;
with the drrrrri–drrrrrra strokes,
    a flood wakes in her hair.

With the third stroke, the hips gyrate;
    with stroke number four, a tempest
in the frill of her gown;
    with the fifth, the body slackens
and the bra loosens.
    And then, I make her dance
as I drum, make her live or die
    with the stroking sticks;
melt and mold her,
    hard metal soften — a Custer.
For I am a very tempestuous trumpeter,
    a Bandmaster.
And again, when I play the cello or the sax,
    in the cabarina's mix
    of devices,
    a conflict arises.

The thread of my flute's melody
    weaves a garland around her body.
Tra la la li la li li,
    the lock opens with the right key.

Nowadays

Saturday afternoon is called happiness. Sunday is off.
Days pass, one at a time, months, years.
The barometer is buoyant at the office —
polished desk, the steno pretty enough
for leers. Wife stays at home
and a mastiff stands chained at the gate.

    How many kinds of Terilene do you know
when I say happiness?
    When it's dark, the wide pond
    is cosy like my cat.
So nowadays,
    my wife thinks that I am not eating
        enough cheese
        and nowadays I notice in the mirror
        when shaving
        that the razor slips out
        of its safety catch.

Repeatedly retreating

Retreating, repeatedly, the Hottentot warrior
suddenly rushes towards the lion.
Such are the dreams which palpitate
in my heart,
like a flood of rumbling lava.
Will my weak heart stop breathing
altogether?
So these days, I avoid looking, even by mistake,
at the pictures of volcanoes.
These days,
waking on some miraculous moonlit night,
I hear the clear neighing of horses,
as thousands of white stallions
come galloping, in a cloud of dust,
into my heart's sanctuary.
And in fear and trembling, I count
intently my ceaseless heartbeats.
As if now, at last, after three clucks,
the lizard on the wall
will be silent for ever.
Yet, for one last time,
I feel like defying dyspepsia,
and munch through cannons, rockets,
smoke, fire, steel.
After repeatedly retreating,
I, a Hottentot warrior,
rush towards the lion.

Before understanding poetry

Somewhat absent minded, while shaving,
this bright morning . . .
at the time, someone was playing
the violin on the radio . . .
at some point . . . confusing
the razor with the fiddle-stick . . .
a shiver in the blood,
a salty taste in the mouth . . .
and then, I can't recall how I . . .
arrived at the hospital,
unconscious . . .
only the smell of disinfectants
and the purposive movements
of the nurses.

If I just look at a bottle of sleeping pills,
my sleep deepens, like thick glue.
And the night can't escape
through the holes in the mosquito net.
And I drag up from down below
deep whiffs of oxygen . . .
I remember my palpitating life, treasured life,
even after seventeen tablets . . .
You, dear sirs, why read such morbid lines,
for now, keeping mum in your seats . . .
I mean before understanding poetry . . .

Bring your hands up to the nostrils . . .
See if you are breathing at all.

Poem to one's mistress

Prone on that red divan,
 you didn't understand
that I was a thirsty deer
 come to the spring.
If you wanted to eat,
 digging into my liver,
I presented it always to your lips.
For your sake,
 I ran against the odds,
as a race horse.
For your kiss, spent
 a half-million dinars,
 playing king.
Or planted five strictly counted kicks
 on someone's deserved behind.
You understood nothing.
 And, metamorphosed
 into an inane submarine,
you left for Mauritius,
 carrying treacle.
 I die of despair . . . you

You understood Nothing —
 deaf and dumb,
 you . . .
 are a bed pan . . . a bright urinal
 in a toilet,
 needing repairs.

SAMAR SEN
(1915–1987)

Samar Sen's lyrics were admired even in the '30s. But he was not just a 'romantic' modernist, as 'An unemployed lover' shows. 'The rhythm of silence' comes from *Samar Sener Kavita*, Calcutta 1977. The rest appeared in *Adhunik Bangla Kavita* (ed. Buddhadev Bose), Calcutta 1973.

Wherever you go

Wherever you go,
in some startled moment's silence,
suddenly you will hear
death's ceremonious
ceaseless
footfall.

And, where would you go
leaving me?
Wherever you go,
from the sky's great emptiness,
Jupiter's keen glance
will fall
on Leda's white breast.

Meghadut

In the next room,
    a girl is crooning
a lullaby
and those languorous cadences
are floating
like shed leaves
    in the air,
occasionally flaring
    like flames
    in the forest
    of a dark sky.

The storm
    before the rains,
after the rains — flood.
    In the rainy season,
when innumerable hearths and homes
    will collapse
    before the endless waters;
when mute animals
    and loquacious men
    will drift together;
    when in the city streets,
famine's volunteers
    will sing in gangs;
    in your mind then
    the luxurious longing
    for union.
You will return to your married lover.
    O sad girl,
what joy do you find in love,
what joy
    in bearing children?

Exile from Paradise

The sea draws to an end.
Today, the tumultuous dark
shakes its wings
like a bird in flight.
    The sea draws to an end.
    There's no deer left
    in the deep forest;
    the birds
    with green feathers
    have died;
    and in the grey
    penumbra of the hills,
    the tumultuous dark
    shakes its wings
    like a bird
    in flight.
    The sea
    draws to an end.
    In the moonlight,
    time's empty desert
    burns.

Separation

Whatever
trembles
hidden
behind the tuberoses,
whatever shivers
in the wordless
depths
of the hills

You're not here yet.
The evening
descends.
The sky's piteous
in the west;
the breeze
redolent
and the murmuring
of the leaves.

Rhythm of silence

Why do you go out
    into the still night?
The sky is moonless, the sky is dark.
A single star shivers
    in the huge darkness.
A single star shivers
    in the wind.

Why do you go out into the still night,
    leaving me alone?
Why stare wordless,
    like a silent stone?
The sky is moonless,
    the sky is dark.
Leaves tremble in the wind
    and behind the deodar tree,
    a star shivers
    and shivers.
Why abandon me
    from the moment of union
to the muteness
    of the parting?

In intermittent flashes,
    why do I know the rhythm
of your silence
    and understand suddenly,
    why night follows
    day
    and the stars shiver
    on their own —
    why in the dark, green life visits
    an earth made of dirt —
    and understand why
    in the still night you leave me
    from the moment of union
    to the muteness of parting.

Unemployed lover

Day after day,
I roam about the Black Market.

        In the morning,
at the water taps, the tired whores
make a commotion;
in the night, I listen
to the ships' horns
from the Kidderpore docks;
at times,
in a tired sort of way,
I think of something
or other.
O god of love,
sleep still keeps off. I pull
at a cigarette.
And sometimes, all eyes,
in the city streets,
I watch the arrogant,
soft breasts
of the Anglo-Indian girls.
        And, at intoxicating midnight,
I occasionally say to myself,
rid me, please, of deathless love,
bring about a new earth
on earth,
wield ready days like steel.
        In the tired tumult
of Calcutta,
in the morning, sleep shatters
and, in the blood, burns
continuously,
the desolation
of a bourgeois civilisation.

SIDHVESWAR SEN
(1930—)

Not always fully appreciated for the resistance his poems offer to easy grasp, due to his Symbolist techniques of ellipsis, syntactic ambiguities, the deliberate rupture of structural continuities, Sen is a subtle and original poet. Although publishing since the late '40s, his first book of poems only appeared in 1980 (*Ghanachanda Muktir Nibid*). The poems in this volume cover the period from 1959 to 1968 and come from his *Sidhveswar Sener Kavita*, 2, Calcutta 1984.

For Pandora, again

I was stunned
when you held open
that lid

The whirl of wind
twisted us around, plague-ridden
tornado — greed-grief-lament

For repressed urges, sustenance

When blood-strife-dread
human defeat

Stunned by venomous fumes
I
kept standing

In that lored penumbra, —
wordless

Until, again, you
shut it close, with startled hands

That gaping, gaping mouth
of primal horror

By then, they had turned everything
topsy-turvy

Only under the shut lid
fallen — hope

Man staked his all on it
and stood, kept standing
for ever

Instants of metamorphosis

An instant or other of the time
of metamorphosis
casts such keen light

One by one the horizon's curves
can be seen suddenly

One by one the complex curves
between the sky and the earth

In the earth's, the sky's
very intimate depths

Or in dormant array
that receives a language to wake again

Who descends into the water

Is metaphor, then, a sunk boat even now

Land on this side or that
I bring her to shore, on this side or that,
She won't move forward

Sometime, of a sudden, salt water entered her

At midnight, she is unstoppable,
Breaks down all directions,
Her nature is not to tarry

In the sky, once again, the clouds
clash —
Who knows, the one who descends
into the water, is a diver.

Would the century listen?

Would the century end, having heard
our pleas?

As far as it streams through darkness,
hugging the banks of being, non-being

As far as Odysseus, broken helm, torn canvas,
you remain on some submerged island, stuck —

Destiny-driven hero,
when will you return, return to this land of Ithaca.

The cock's crow

'Verily, I say unto thee,
that this night, before the
cock crow, thou shalt deny
me thrice.'
St. Matthew, XXVI, 34

Afterwards, going out to the gate
I covered my face
Three times that cock's crow, thrice,
Thrice that

My remorse
Because it was thrice, three times

Do I deny
Or affirm

Not for any compassion, that self-
Reproach, in this reproachful dark
Only, perhaps, at some behest

O thrice forgiveness, you will mount the triple rood
Hands and feet pierced and the heart, son
Made human

And this threshold's weight, now
On me, breaks

My fealty, behind you
Follows substantiality

Even then, bent down with weight,
I am sense-forsaken shadow,
Renunciator, sham,
Standing at the gate's threshold

Outside, the cock crows
True or false
That cry?

The chief priest's hand — (whose hand
In Iscariot's
Grasp)
Over you stops

Unfriendly city
And bitter smelling mouths
Rhyming obscenely or otherwise

I watch history, history
In self-sacrifice, all devouring,
In destruction, mute
And full of words

My remorse, this
Of bearing mere testimony, head bent,
At this procession of martyrs
At Golgotha

Merely witnessing, witnessing, destitute
Incompetent
— may be chilled by your injunction

I did not deny you.

KABITA SINHA

(1932—)

Kabita Sinha's is a powerful new voice which projects feminist themes, without losing lyric authenticity. She works for the All India Radio. Her poems have appeared in various magazines. 'Suntouched', a fine achievement, came out in *Ek Bacharer Sreshtha Kavita* (1974), Calcutta 1975. 'I am that girl' was first delivered as an address at Bethune College's Centenary and then published in *Bethune College Centenary Volume (1879–1979)*, Calcutta 1980.

Sun touched

This fierce riding sun,
harsh, exact; upturned faces;
eyes on eyes;
in a dazzle of display,
the sight is blinded
by an infatuation
with sun light.
The heart's wick burns.
The gullet, the intestines,
the air passage
burn, burn without oil.
The citified bodies
in blouse, petticoat, chemise,
all brown and pink
arils of colour, peel off
layer by layer.
Like spathes of plantain,
first iridescent
then pale, anaemic.
Like bunched bamboos
slowly sunward
opening up shoots, until
they are white, conchlike fists.

Sunlight, countless needles,
fills ceaselessly
the minuscule gaps,
as if mere pin chushions.
Oh, how flexed arms open
to the roots and the talcum
clots on her breasts.
Each her atom pitifully begs
for the unadulterate dark.
The locked thighs
open on their hinges
as the sun-baked wind stirs
each her cell
and infuses her blood,
somehow, with adultery.
Somehow, the sun whirls
in secret

blood's bubbles,
the ova, the sperm,
and makes them exploding
bubbles of the sun,
innumerable, pure.
Oh, how he arouses her
and lets her drift
and drift,
his warmth melting
beneath her follicles,
spreading tinsel of gold
even after sun down.
Now, on a cold night
she burns
in hidden exultation.

I am that girl

I am that girl.
That girl at whose birth no conch shells
rang out,
who from birth is a prisoner
of the astrologer's chart,
whose ascendant has been scoured
for the nodes of the moon — not
for her own sake, no —
    for her father's sake,
    for her brother's,
    for her prospective bridegroom's,
    for her son's sake.
But no one ever spoke of that mother
    from whose womb
    I took birth.

I am that girl,
    who from birth, is dedicated as sacrifice
    at the marriage-altar,
    whose appearance —
    eyes, nose, mouth, skin, hair,
    complexion,
    are the sole items
    for bargaining.
    Dark or light skinned,
    with a flat nose or sharp,
    tall or short,
    eyes sunk and tiny or wide and long
    like an idol's?

What's not in her head
    causes everyone anxiety,
but no one bothers about what's inside.
    I am that girl
    who has heard from childhood
that one must not speak loud,
    mustn't run,
    mustn't shout,
    mustn't laugh
    and that even tears must be shed
    in secret.

I am that girl who mustn't say
    I am hungry,
    I am sleepy,
    I don't want,
    I am tired,
    I can't any more,
    I can't any more.

I am that girl
    who has been handed a doll to play with,
    to pet the doll,
    to set up a doll's house.

I am that girl
    who, dreaming of a pre-historic
    moonlit night,
    still starts with terror.
    I have seen blood stream
    at my hair's parting,
    marked by the stone and axe
    of that half-demon,
    half-man.
    I have seen him drag me away
    by the iron bangle
    on my wrist.
    From one clan to another, from birth to birth,
    like looted property —
    I have borne the awareness
    of that toll of virility.

Again, waking from the dream,
I have seen women
carefully putting on vermillion
at their hair's parting
and steel bangles on their wrists . . .

I am that girl
who, in some past century,
was wedded at five to some moribund man,
being one of three hundred and sixty five wives
of some noble Brahmin,
was proud
in her husband's pride.

An uncomprehending ten year old,
on the widow's fasting day,
I have thirsted,
licked the earthen floor
of my punishment cell
and died.
Bearing children, one after another,
I have fallen down
on my face, from blood-loss,
in the confinement room.
I have died flaming,
as a suttee.

I could not understand
that in my vulnerability,
the male's maleness
lies in ambush.
I could not understand that I was wrong
to point out my lover's spelling mistakes
in his love letter,
that one shouldn't show one's skill
at work.

I did not understand
    that if I wanted to be a poet,
my friends would say,
'That isn't poetry,
but mere verse.'
I couldn't understand
that at the edges of the twenty first century,
this male-dominated earth
is unprepared for women of intelligence.
That even abroad, talented women
in inane costumes
still date boys.
Because men never stand for intelligence
keener than their own.

    I am that girl
    who has seen how a woman
    becomes a mere wench,
    successful wives
    walk away from their nature,

getting shinier
than cultivated,
in all that sparkle of Benarasi sarees,
the emeralds and diamonds
of their ornaments
outshining
their minds.

I am that girl.
You know, I am that girl
who, now for several years, has committed
blunder after blunder
and then blundered again.
I did not realise
that I am not supposed to be competent.

That I must simper, in a childish voice,
'Well, could you tell me which bus
goes to Bethune College?'
Straight-away,
like any young man,
I used to board
78 C.

I didn't realise
that on the bus, if one stood straight
while hanging on to the overhead rod,
the gentlemen, in the seats
reserved for the ladies,
would never give me a place,
that if I swayed,
as if unable to keep my balance,
my femininity would receive full marks.

But, having come so far this way
I can't retrace my steps.
Now I am allergic
to face powder
and the lipstick tastes
so good
that I quite lick it up
if I put it on.
After so long,

I can't begin
the ritual of coquettishness.
Because I don't want to return
towards the dark,
do I want to walk over
insult's burning cinders?
I want to go
in the direction of sorrow:

I salute the first fire
known as the Primer
and those men/women
who, mutually purified by fire,
groping in the darkness
of the nineteenth century,
lit the flame of knowledge
and in this my one birth
have opened the doors
on my previous incarnations.

Today, moving towards being
myself,
I cast away
the paste jewellery of a marriage
bought with dowry,
the Benarasi sarees
of conventions,
the preparation of beetle leaves
with the condiment of tobacco —
to keep me distracted,
the pompous titles of my father,
husband, father-in-law
to make me feel weighty.

Today, I leave ease behind
for love,
the slave's feast
for my earned bread and water.
To stay awake, I abandon the siesta,
for pain, abandon happiness,
for knowledge, blindness.
for joy, success, for the intoxicating nectar,
treasures.

The noble flame of knowledge burns
in my hands, for those who seek.
I am that girl, whom you must recognise
when looking at yourselves
in the mirror.

Other Titles from
FOREST BOOKS

International Poetry Series

THE NAKED MACHINE Selected poems of Matthías Johannessen.
Translated from the *Icelandic* by Marshall Brement.
(Forest/Almenna bokáfélagid)
0 948259 44 2 cloth £7.95   0 948259 43 4 paper £5.95   96pages   Illustrated

ON THE CUTTING EDGE Selected poems of Justo Jorge Padrón.
Translated from the *Spanish* by Louis Bourne.
0 948259 42 6 paper £8.95   176 pages

ROOM WITHOUT WALLS Selected poems of Bo Carpelan.
Translated from the *Swedish* by Anne Born.
0 948259 08 6 paper £7.95   144 pages.   Illustrated

CALL YOURSELF ALIVE? The love poems of Nina Cassian.
Translated from the *Romanian* by Andrea Deletant and
Brenda Walker. Introduction by Fleur Adcock.
0 948259 38 8 paper £6.95.   96 pages.   Illustrated

A VANISHING EMPTINESS Selected poems of Willem M. Roggeman.
Edited by Yann Lovelock. Translated from the *Dutch*.
0 948259 51 5 paper £7.95   112 pages.   Illustrated

PORTRAIT OF THE ARTIST AS AN ABOMINABLE SNOWMAN
Selected poems of Gabriel Rosenstock translated from the
Irish by Michael Hartnett. New Poems translated by Jason Sommer.
0 948259 56 6 paper £7.95   112 pages   Dual text

LAND AND PEACE Selected poems of Desmond Egan.
Translated *into Irish* by Michael Hartnett, Gabriel Rosenstock,
Douglas Sealey and Tomas MacSiomoin. Dual text.
0 948259 64 7 paper £7.95   112 pages

THE EYE IN THE MIRROR Selected poems of Takis Varvitsiotis.
Translated from the *Greek* by Kimon Friar. (Forest/Paratiritis)
0 948259 59 0 paper £8.95   160 pages

THE WORLD AS IF Selected poems of Uffe Harder.
Translated from the *Danish* by John F. Deane and Uffe Harder.
(Dedalus/Forest)
0 948259 76 0 paper £4.95   80 pages

SPRING TIDE Selected poems of Pia Tafdrup.
Translated from the *Danish* by Anne Born.
0 948259 55 8 paper £7.95   96 pages

SNOW AND SUMMERS Selected poems of Solveig von Schoultz.
Translated from *Finland/Swedish* by Anne Born.
Introduction by Bo Carpelan. Arts Council funded.
0 948259 52 3 paper £7.95   112 pages

FOOTPRINTS OF THE WIND Selected poems of Mateja Matevski.
Translated from the *Macedonian* by Ewald Osers.
Introduction by Robin Skelton. Arts Council funded.
0 948259 41 8 paper £6.95   96 pages. Illustrated

ARIADNE'S THREAD An anthology of contemporary Polish women poets. Translated from the *Polish* by Susan Bassnett and Piotr Kuhiwczak. UNESCO collection of representative works.
0 948259 45 0 paper £6.95   96 pages

POETS OF BULGARIA An anthology of contemporary Bulgarian poets.
Edited by William Meredith. Introduction by Alan Brownjohn.
0 948259 39 6 paper £6.95   112 pages

FIRES OF THE SUNFLOWER Selected poems by Ivan Davidkov.
Translated from the *Bulgarian* by Ewald Osers.
0 948259 48 5 paper £6.95   96 pages.   Illustrated

STOLEN FIRE Selected poems by Lyubomir Levchev.
Translated from the *Bulgarian* by Ewald Osers.
Introduction by John Balaban.
UNESCO collection of representative works.
0 948259 04 3 paper £6.95   112 pages.   Illustrated

AN ANTHOLOGY OF CONTEMPORARY ROMANIAN POETRY
Translated by Andrea Deletant and Brenda Walker.
0 9509487 4 8 paper £6.95   112 pages.

GATES OF THE MOMENT Selected poems of Ion Stoica.
Translated from the *Romanian* by Brenda Walker and Andrea Deletant. Dual text with cassette.
0 9509487 0 5 paper £6.95   126 pages   Cassette £3.50 plus VAT

SILENT VOICES An anthology of contemporary Romanian women poets. Translated by Andrea Deletant and Brenda Walker.
0 948259 03 5 paper £8.95   172 pages

EXILE ON A PEPPERCORN Selected poems of Mircea Dinescu.
Translated from the *Romanian* by Andrea Deletant and Brenda Walker.
0 948259 00 0 paper £7.95   96 pages.   Illustrated

LET'S TALK ABOUT THE WEATHER Selected poems of Marin Sorescu
Translated from the *Romanian* by Andrea Deletant and Brenda Walker.
0 9509487 8 0 paper £6.95   96 pages

THE ROAD TO FREEDOM Poems and Prose Poems by Geo Milev
Translated from the *Bulgarian* by Ewald Osers.
UNESCO Collection of representative works
0 948259 40 X paper £6.95   96 pages   Illustrated

IN CELEBRATION OF MIHAI EMINESCU Selected poems and extracts translated from the *Romanian* by Brenda Walker and Horia Florian Popescu. Illustrated by Sabin Balaşa.
0 948259 62 0   Limited edition £20   176 pages

THROUGH THE NEEDLE'S EYE Selected poems of Ion Milos.
Translated from the *Romanian* by Brenda Walker and Ion Milos.
0 948259 61 2 paper £6.95   96 pages.   Illustrated

JOUSTS OF APHRODITE Poems collected from the Greek Anthology Book V
Translated from the *Greek* into modern English by Michael Kelly.
0 948259 05 1 cloth £6.95 0 948259 34 5 paper £4.95 96 pages

FISH-RINGS ON WATER Selected poems by Katherine Gallagher, the *Australian* poet. Introduced by Peter Porter.
0 948259 75 2 paper £6.95 96 pages Illustrated

PIED POETS An anthology of Romanian Transylvanian and Danube poets writing in German. Translated from the *German* by Robert Elsie.
Dual text English/German. Arts Council funded
0 948259 77 9 paper £9.95 192 pages

LOVE SONNETS OF THE RENAISSANCE
Translated from the *French, Italian* and *Spanish* and *Portuguese* by Laurence Kitchin.
0 948259 60 4 paper £6.95 96 pages Dual text

BEFORE WE WERE STRANGERS Poems by the *American* poet Nadya Aisenberg.
Introduced by Sylvia Kantaris.
0 948259 81 7 paper £6.95 96 pages

WASTELANDS OF FIRE Poems by Ku Sang.
Translated from the *Korean* by Anthony Teague.
0 948259 82 5 paper £7.95 144 pages

CLOSED CIRCUIT by Shadab Vajdi.
Translated from the *Persian* by Lotfali Kohonji and introduced by Peter Avery.
0 948259 78 7 paper £6.95 96 pages

STEP HUMAN INTO THIS WORLD Poems by Olaf Munzberg.
Translated from the *German* by Mitch Cohen.
0 948259 53 1 paper £6.95 96 pages

ENCHANTING BEASTS An anthology of Finnish women poets.
Translated from the *Finnish* and the *Swedish* by Kirsti Simonsuuri.
0 948259 68 X paper £8.95 160 pages

International Drama Series

THE THIRST OF THE SALT MOUNTAIN Three plays by Marin Sorescu (Jonah, The Verger, and the Matrix) Translated from the *Romanian* by Andrea Deletant and Brenda Walker.
0 9509487 5 6 paper £7.95 124 pages. Illustrated

VLAD DRACULA THE IMPALER A play by Marin Sorescu
Translated from the *Romanian* by Dennis Deletant.
0 948259 07 8 paper £6.95 112 pages. Illustrated

International Short Story Series

RUNNING TO THE SHROUDS Six sea stories of Konstantin Stanyukovich.
Translated from the *Russian* by Neil Parsons.
0 948259 06 X paper £6.95 112 pages.

HEARTWORK Stories of Solveig von Schoultz.
Translated from *Finland/Swedish* by Marlaine Delargy and Joan Tate. Introduction by Bo Carpelan.
0 948259 50 7 paper £7.95 144 pages

THICKHEAD AND OTHER STORIES by Haldun Taner.
Translated from the *Turkish* by Geoffrey Lewis.
UNESCO collection of representative works.
0 948259 58 2 paper £8.95 176 pages

YOUTH WITHOUT YOUTH and other Novellas by Mircea Eliade.
Edited and with an introduction by Matei Calinescu.
Translated from the *Romanian* by MacLinscott Ricketts.
0 948259 74 4 paper £12.95 328 pages

A WOMAN'S HEART Stories by Jordan Yovkov.
Translated from the *Bulgarian* by John Burnip.
0 948259 54 X paper £9.95 208 pages

THE SEER AND OTHER STORIES by Jonas Lie.
Translated from the *Norwegian* by Brian Morton and Richard Trevor.
0 948259 65 5 paper £9.95 208 pages

THE TALISMAN Stories and poems by Ganga Prasad Vimal.
Edited by Wendy Wright. G.L.A. funded.
0 948259 57 4 paper £9.95 208 pages Dual text English/Hindi.

PREPARATIONS FOR FLIGHT and other Swedish stories.
Translated from the *Swedish* by Robin Fulton
0 948259 66 3 paper £8.95 176 pages